WORCESTER IN 50 BUILDINGS

JAMES DINN

AMBERLEY

About the Author

James Dinn spent the first half of his archaeological career in field archaeology, mainly in Wales and the western Midlands. Since 1997 he has been the Archaeological Officer at Worcester City Council, where he developed the Worcester Urban Archaeological Database and has overseen excavations on sites of all periods from the Mesolithic to the Second World War. He is fascinated by the hidden quirks of historic buildings, and by the evidence they embody for past lives and livelihoods. James lives in Malvern with his family.

First published 2018

Amberley Publishing, The Hill, Stroud
Gloucestershire GL5 4EP

www.amberley-books.com

British Library Cataloguing in Publication Data.
A catalogue record for this book is available from the British Library.

ISBN 978 1 4456 8051 4 (print)
ISBN 978 1 4456 8052 1 (ebook)

Origination by Amberley Publishing.
Printed in Great Britain.

Contents

Introduction

Worcester is well known as a quintessentially English medieval cathedral city, though its origins go back even earlier than the Roman settlement indicated by the -cester name. When the Romans arrived in around AD 55, there had already been a defended settlement here for some 800 years. They found an Iron Age earthwork on the east bank of the Severn, whose rampart and ditch was reused as a defence for the ironworking town of Vertis. The Roman town was characterised by kilns, smelting furnaces and slag heaps, and its streets were quite literally paved with iron (slag), though occasional finds of mosaic and architectural stonework show that it was not all industrial grime.

The Iron Age earthwork is key to Worcester's existence. It was still very evident in 680, when a cathedral for the Anglo-Saxon kingdom of the Hwicce was planted at its centre. The High Street alignment had Roman origins, but the Mercian establishment of a defended burh against the Danes in the 990s brought it inside an extended defence and gave it commercial impetus.

The city centre from Diglis.

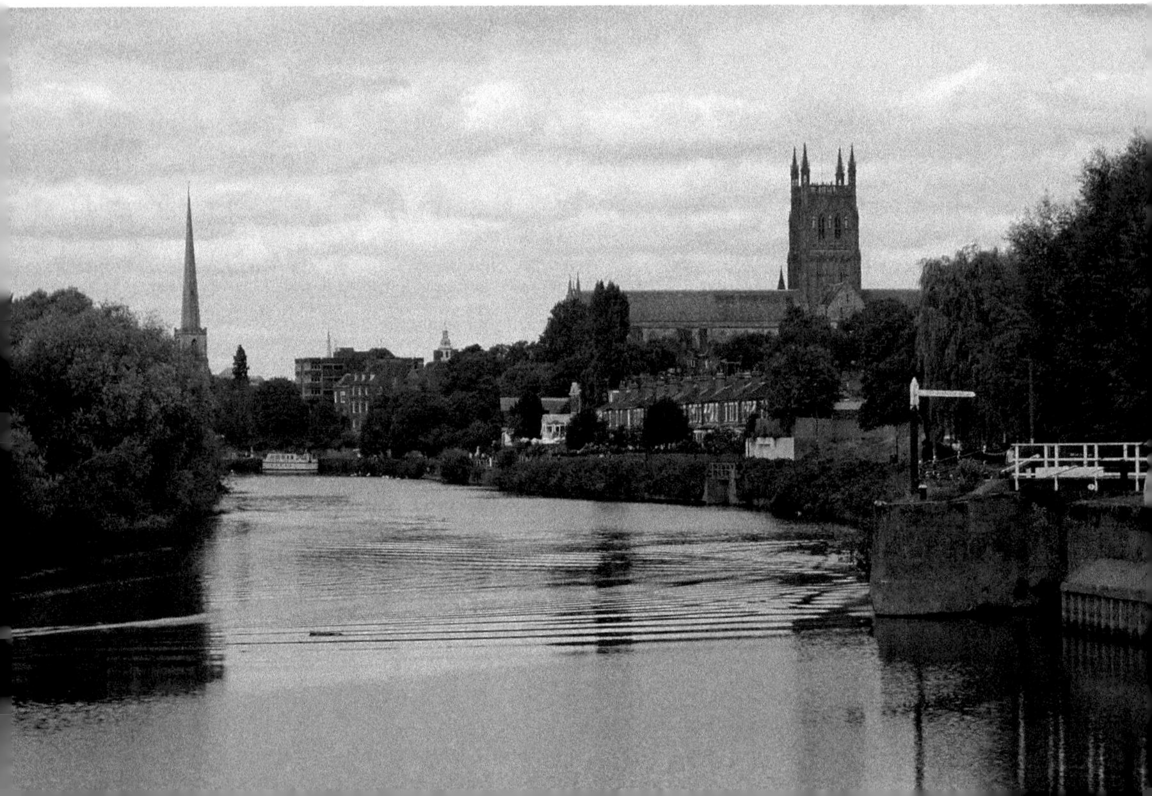

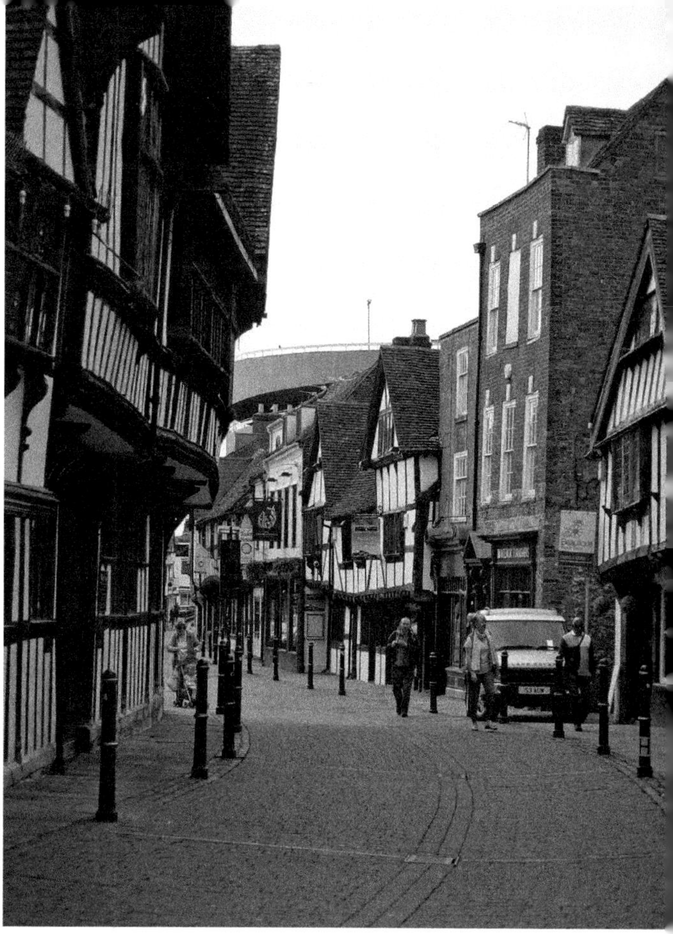

Historic buildings in Friar Street.

After the Norman Conquest, a castle secured control of the city, while Wulfstan rebuilt the cathedral. A century later, a new defensive perimeter was established, which was to define the city centre for some 800 years. The medieval walls enclosed a thriving city with at least ten parish churches and four monastic houses. Most of those buildings were stone, while the majority of domestic buildings were timber framed, a pattern which was to continue until after 1700. City Ordinances of 1467 required chimney stacks to be stone and roofs to be covered with clay tiles, and occasionally tiles from this period can still be found on roofs.

Outside the walls were suburbs at Sidbury, Lowesmoor, Foregate and St John's. These bore the brunt of destruction during the seventeenth-century Civil War; many of the suburbs were deliberately levelled by the defenders, and the residents had to seek shelter within the walls.

Ceramic and textile industries were important in medieval Worcester, and were joined later by glove making, the production of vinegar, sauce and porcelain, and heavier industries including engineering. Farming products were traded in the many markets including the Hopmarket.

In the eighteenth century there was more than a veneer of Georgian elegance, with many new brick houses, and four of the medieval churches rebuilt, but the centre became increasingly crowded with housing in courts behind the frontages. From the early nineteenth century Worcester began to expand, with fine brick and stucco houses in new suburban developments well outside the walls.

The coming of the canal in 1815 and the railway in 1850 were important for industry and trade, and started to pull the city further to the east. New streets of artisan and working-class housing from the mid-nineteenth century reduced the pressure on the city centre somewhat, though many of the courts degenerated into slums.

Attempts to improve housing conditions included a small garden city before the First World War, but it was not until the late 1920s that substantial strides were made. Worcester's growth to the east continued, later fuelled by the building of the M5. The city centre courts were cleared in the mid-twentieth century, and the residents of whole neighbourhoods moved to new estates in Dines Green, Tolladine and Warndon.

Worcester is able to look to the future while keeping strong links with its heritage and origins. Its skyline is still marked not only by a fine array of medieval and Georgian towers, as well as many Victorian and Edwardian cupolas and turrets, but also by the buildings of the university, a new creation in the first years of the twenty-first century.

Key

1. The Guildhall
2. The Golden Lion, High Street
3. St Helen's Church, Fish Street
4. Cathedral Square (Lychgate Centre)
5. Worcester Cathedral
6. The Monastic Precinct, Worcester Cathedral
7. Worcester Castle
8. Michael Baker Boathouse (King's School)
9. Royal Worcester Porcelain, Severn Street
10. The Commandery
11. Sidbury Gate and the City Walls
12. Fownes Hotel, City Walls Road
13. Tudor House, Friar Street
14. The Greyfriars, Friar Street
15. Nash House, New Street
16. King Charles House, Cornmarket and New Street
17. Nos 18–20 Silver Street (the Old Infirmary)
18. Hill, Evans & Co. Vinegar Works: the New Filling Hall
19. Queen Elizabeth House, The Trinity
20. St Swithun's Church, Church Street
21. No. 61 Broad Street (Cupola House)
22. Lloyds Bank, The Cross
23. Corn Exchange, Angel Street
24. The Hopmarket, The Foregate
25. Berkeley's Hospital, The Foregate
26. The Hop Pickers, Sansome Street
27. The Old Rackets Court, Sansome Walk
28. Museum and Art Gallery (Victoria Institute), Foregate Street
29. The Shirehall, Foregate Street
30. Austin House, Castle Street
31. Worcester Infirmary (University of Worcester)
32. The Paul Pry, The Butts
33. The Hive
34. Worcester Bridge
35. Huntingdon Hall (Countess of Huntingdon's Chapel), Deansway
36. The Glovers' Needle (St Andrew's Spire)
37. The Old Palace
38. Kays Building, The Tything
39. Britannia Square
40. St George's Church, Barbourne
41. Gheluvelt Park and Memorial Arch
42. Northwick Cinema, Ombersley Road
43. Shrub Hill Station and Waiting Rooms
44. Shrub Hill Engine Works
45. St Nicholas', Warndon
46. Battenhall Mount
47. St John in Bedwardine
48. St Cuthbert's Chapel
49. Powick Old Bridge
50. Powick Mills

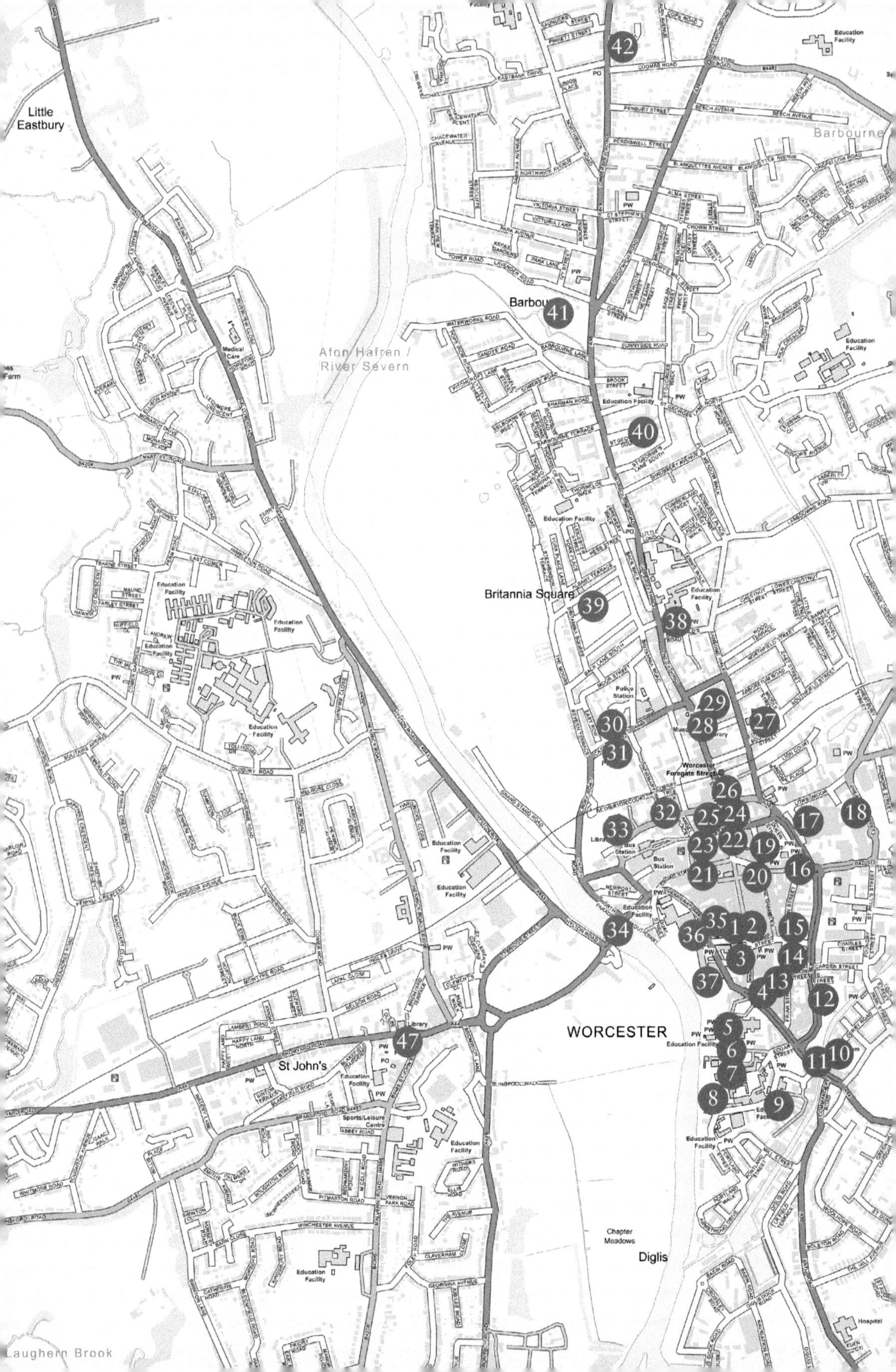

Little Eastbury
Barbourne
Barbou
Afon Hafren / River Severn
Britannia Square
WORCESTER
St John's
Chapter Meadows
Diglis
Laughern Brook
Worcester Foregate Street
Bus Station
Police Station
Library
Education Facility
Medical Care
Sports/Leisure Centre
Hospital
1
2
3
4
5
6
7
8
9
10
11
12
13
14
15
16
17
18
19
20
21
22
23
24
25
26
27
28
29
30
31
32
33
34
35
36
37
38
39
40
41
42
47

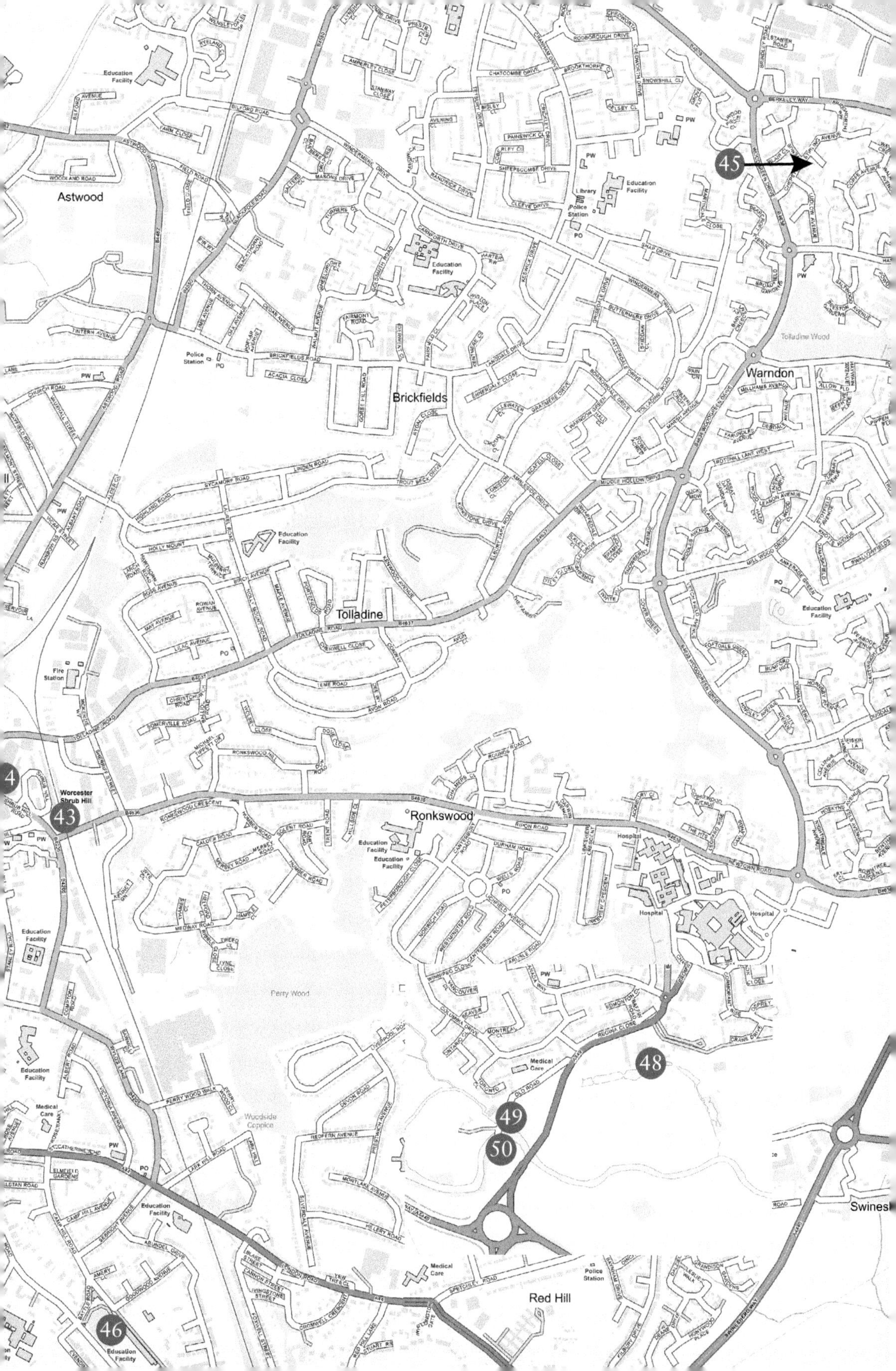

Astwood
Brickfields
Tolladine
Warndon
Ronkswood
Red Hill
Perry Wood
Woodside Coppice
Tolladine Wood
Worcester Shrub Hill
45
43
46
48
49
50

The 50 Buildings

1. The Guildhall

Worcester's Guildhall is one of the grandest town halls of the eighteenth century. Valentine Green in 1764 claimed that it was 'justly esteemed the most elegant and magnificent of the kind in the kingdom'. It is hard to believe that in the 1870s the Queen Anne building came close to demolition, only saved, it is said, by Mayor John Noake's casting vote. It was planned to replace it with a Gothic town hall. An architectural competition drew entries from the likes of Alfred Waterhouse (architect of the Natural History Museum), but Sir George Gilbert Scott and others lobbied for restoration.

Archaeological excavation has revealed remains of a Roman building below the cellars, as well as stone foundations of the medieval (timber-framed) guildhall buildings. The site was probably first laid out in the 990s as part of the Anglo-Saxon burh.

The Guildhall was rebuilt in 1721–24, with the three-storey wings, less grand and always intended for letting, following in 1725 and 1727. It has been claimed

The main front of the Guildhall. (Chris Dobbs)

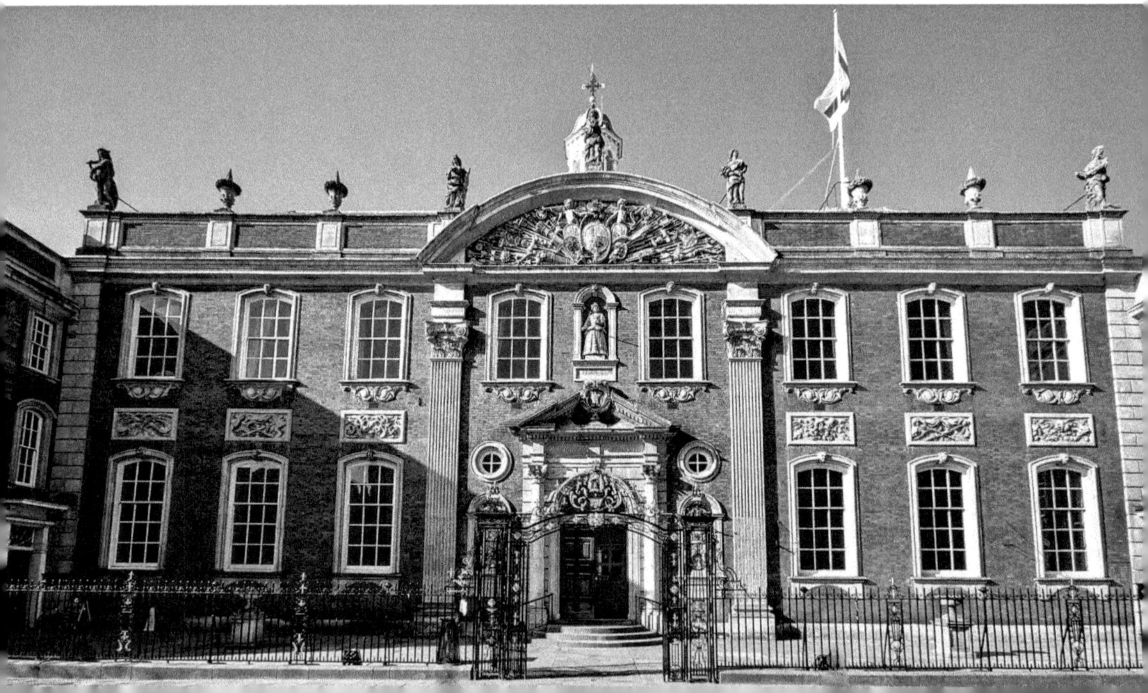

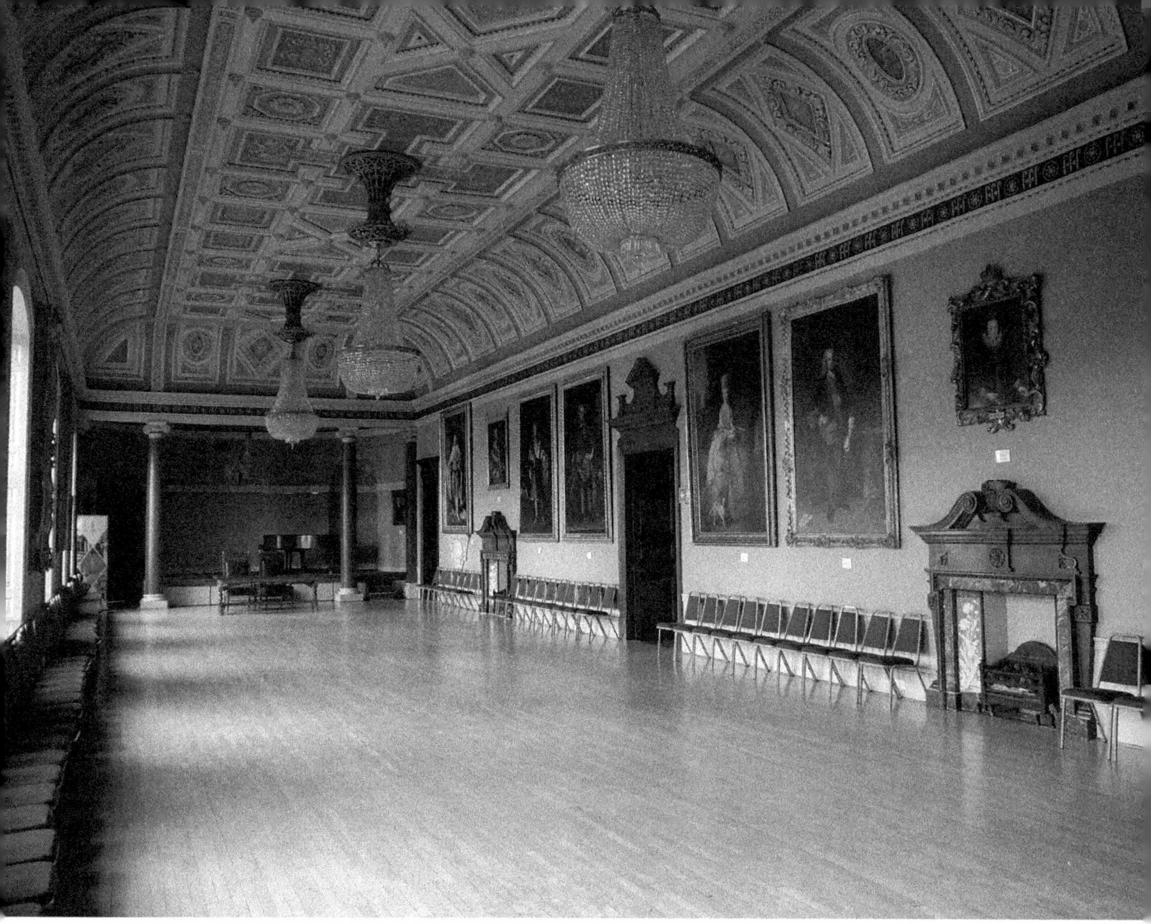

The Assembly Room.

as the work of Thomas White, but while he was certainly responsible for the pediment carving, there is no evidence that he designed the building.

The main two-storey façade is of brick with heavily moulded stone window surrounds, plinth and cornice. On either side of the main doorway are 'stodgy' (Pevsner) seventeenth-century statues of Charles I and II in niches, with Queen Anne above. The demonic face immediately over the door is said to be of Cromwell (there is a legend that he sold his soul to the Devil before the Battle of Worcester, in return for seven years as ruler). Full-height stop-fluted Corinthian pilasters are surmounted by White's 'Roman trophy' pediment with its extravagant display of weaponry as well as cherubs. The parapet is decorated with sculpted figures of Justice, Peace, Plenty, Chastisement and Hercules (representing Labour).

The main wing of the Guildhall has single large spaces at the front. The functional Lower Hall is undecorated, and houses the roll of honour of Worcester's war dead. For many centuries the Guildhall was the seat of city justice, and behind the hall were two courts (one now converted into the mayor's parlour). There were cells in the cellars. A grand staircase leads to the Assembly Room, which is highly decorated. The apses at either end (by George Byfield) have Adam-style details, and there are late Victorian painted ceilings (part of the major restoration by Scott and city architect Henry Rowe in 1878–80). Also at this level is the Council Chamber, with art deco lanterns.

The ornate railings to the forecourt were installed in 1751 (said to be by Bakewell of Derby) and carefully renewed in 1880 by Letheram, using record photographs taken the previous year as a guide to the restoration.

2. The Golden Lion, High Street

Facing the Guildhall, the Golden Lion was built as a merchant's house with shop, in a prime location on the High Street, by the High Cross. With four storeys and cellars, the building makes the most of the limited street frontage in one of the most expensive areas of the medieval city. Now a coffee bar, the Golden Lion was a pub from the sixteenth century until the late 1970s.

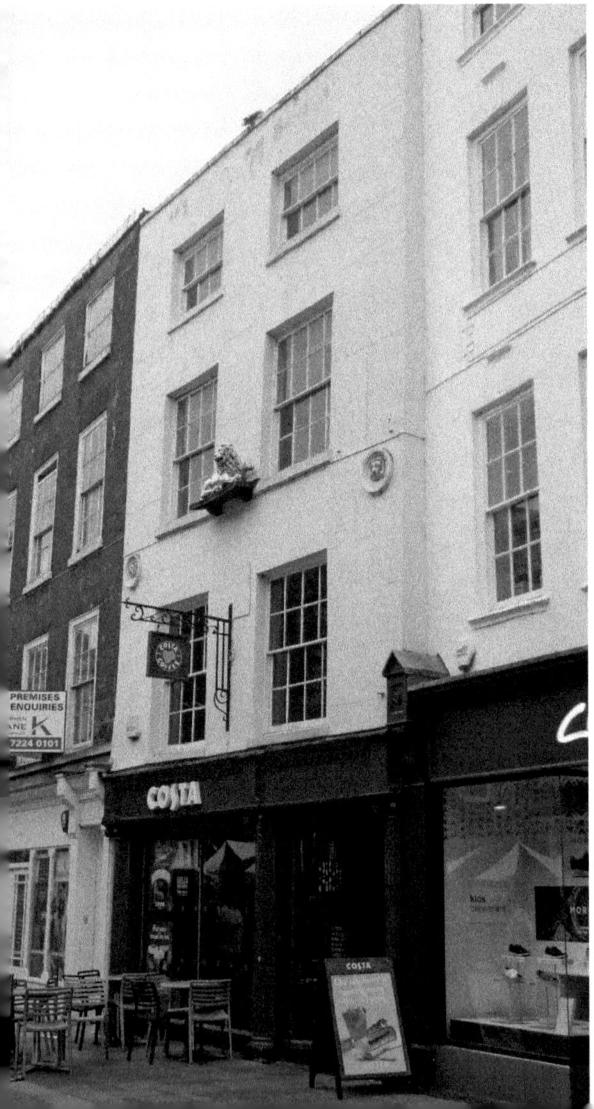

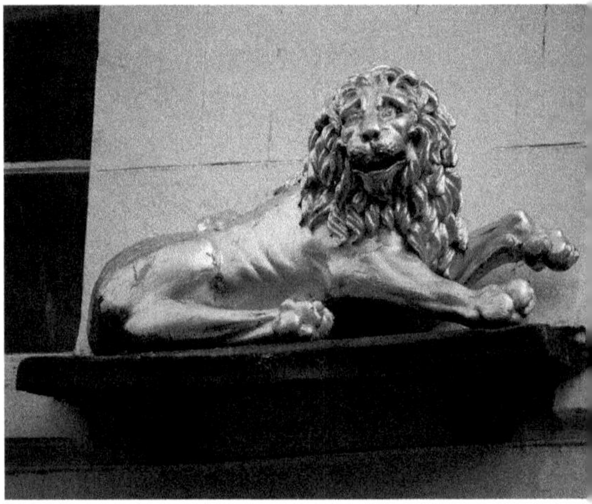

Above: The Golden Lion.

Left: The High Street façade of the Golden Lion.

Built in around 1400, the building is timber framed with a two-bay open first-floor hall with tiebeam and wind-braced roof, which has clasped purlins. To the front, jetties and gables were probably removed around 1700. A stucco façade was added in the early nineteenth century, and is still adorned with the pub sign, a fully three-dimensional gilded lion.

Stone cellars run under most of the building. These would have been used for both storage and trading, entered down steps from the street, which was then at a lower level than now.

Restoration by F. W. B. Charles in 1988 involved the replacement of many original timbers, but successfully reinstated the character of the medieval open hall, which is now accessible to the public.

A well known feature of the Golden Lion is the face mask on the wall. This is said to be the death mask of William Guise, a Worcester tailor, who on 29 August 1651 (five days before the Battle of Worcester) overheard Royalists here making plans for an attack, and informed the Parliamentary side. For this, he was hanged from the sign of the Golden Cross Inn in Broad Street, and it is claimed that the Golden Lion is haunted by the ghosts of his wife and child.

3. St Helen's Church, Fish Street

Medieval on the inside but largely Victorian on the outside, St Helen's Church is in the very centre of the city and is known as Worcester's 'mother church'. In 1092 the parish included what is now outer Worcester (St John's, St Peter the Great,

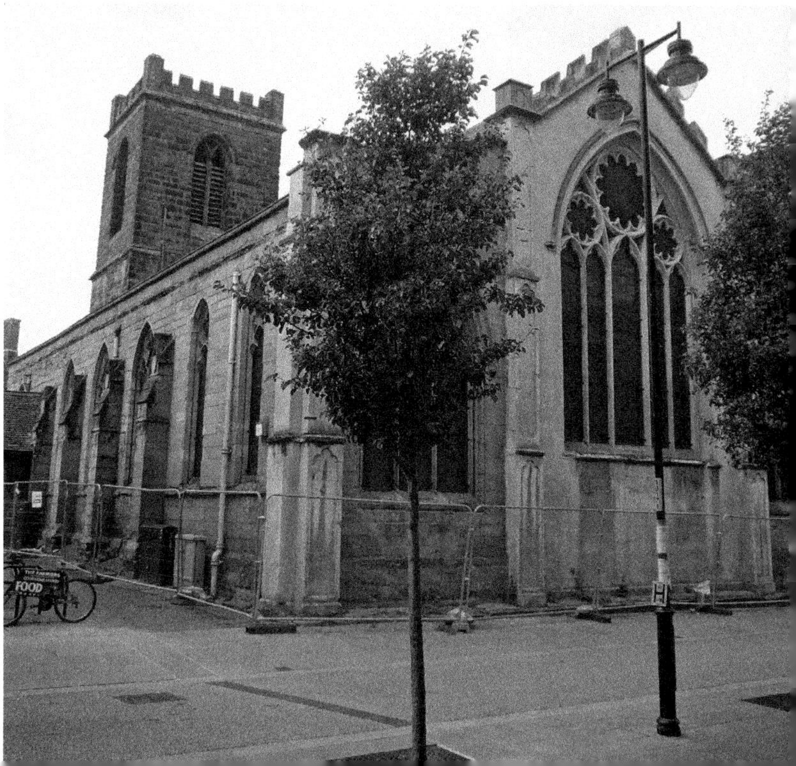

St Helen's Church from the High Street.

Claines and Warndon), and extended to Knightwick in the west and White Ladies Aston in the east. It was believed then that St Helen's predated the foundation of the cathedral. This suggests that it was a minster church. St Helen's and the nearby St Alban's (now Maggs Day Centre) are sited on top of the Roman town's rampart. Both churches are dedicated to Roman saints: St Helen was the mother of the emperor Constantine, while St Alban was the first British martyr. Archaeologists have speculated that there could be a Roman building on the site, perhaps even a temple.

Several of Worcester's churches have their main façade at the east end. St Helen's faces the busy High Street. A Georgian Gothic remodelling (1718) included two eastern doorways to the High Street. These disappeared in Preedy's restoration of 1857–63, when this wall was encased in Cotswold stone. Aston Webb rebuilt the south aisle and part of the east end in 1879–80 and added the timber porch. He also designed one of his signature mosaic floors (others can be seen at Claines and St George's, Barbourne).

The low sandstone tower at the west end is still a significant feature on Worcester's skyline. The upper parts were rebuilt by Collingwood in 1820–21, while the lowest stage seems to be medieval.

The heavily leaning north wall preserves some thirteenth-century stonework, but most of the red sandstone interior, including the fine six-bay arcades, is in the Perpendicular style of the mid-fifteenth century.

The furnishings were removed to make way for the church's twentieth-century uses as a canteen in the Second World War and as the County Record Office from 1957 to 2002. A fine collection of monuments survives, however, including a large and elaborate one to John Nash, city alderman, and a twentieth-century tablet commemorating Dud Dudley, illegitimate son of Lord Dudley, a Royalist commander during the Civil War and later an innovative ironmaster.

4. Cathedral Square (Lychgate Centre)

The city centre of Worcester suffered some extreme shocks in the 1960s including widespread demolitions. While these may have brought Worcester into the twentieth century, it was at the cost of some of the city's oldest buildings, and here a whole street.

The Lychgate Centre, now Cathedral Square, was the earlier (1965–67) and more architecturally interesting of Worcester's two 1960s shopping precincts, the other being the Blackfriars (now Friary Mall). Requiring the demolition of all of Lich Street, much of College Street and the southern end of High Street, the new centre provided a shopping precinct, department store, supermarket, hotel, flats, offices, a multistorey car park and even a church. The road system was remodelled, with a large roundabout in front of the cathedral.

What made way for this included some fine timber-framed buildings in Lich Street, the medieval Lychgate – the last remaining cathedral lychgate in

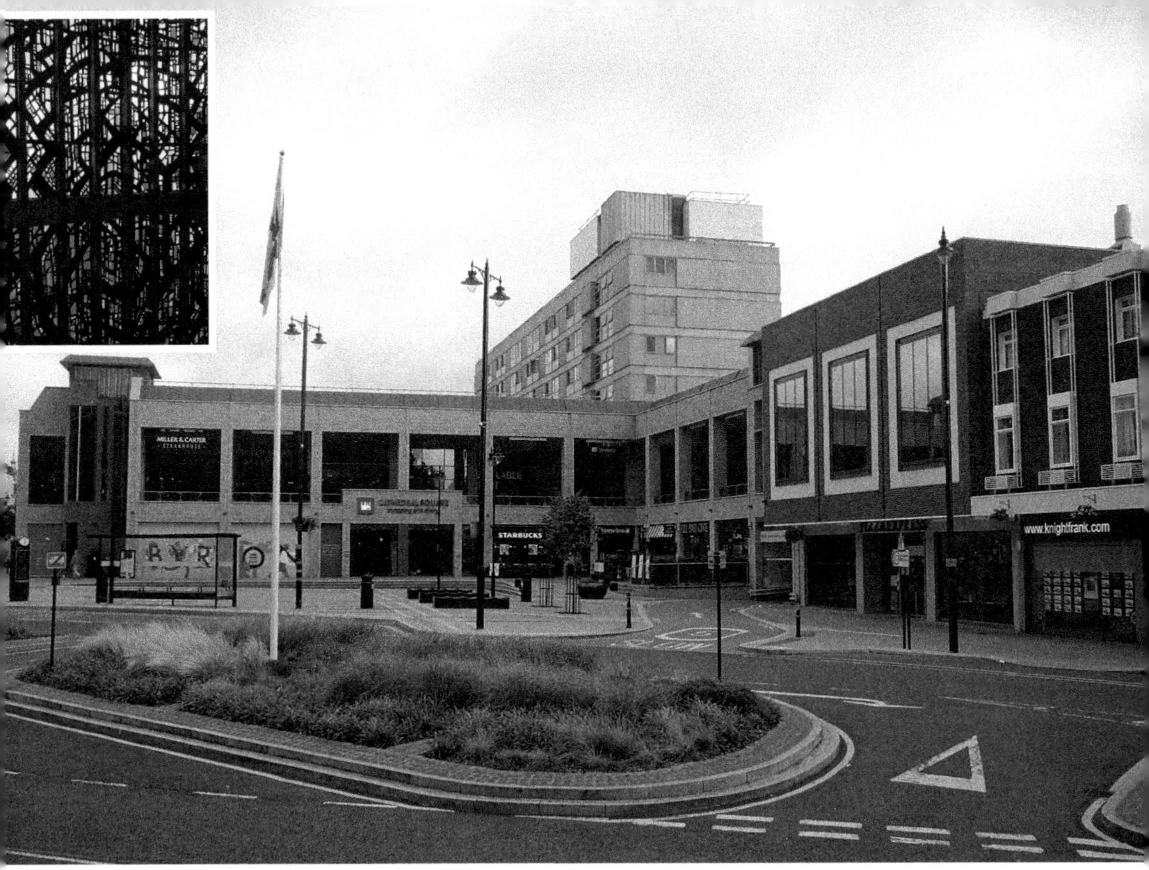

The remodelled Cathedral Square.

Inset: Dalle de verre window at St Andrew's Methodist Church.

Britain – and the Elgar family's music shop in High Street (now marked by a plaque). Many of the buildings had been allowed to deteriorate so much that demolition was welcomed in the name of slum clearance.

Also lost were archaeological remains beneath the surface, to make way for huge basements. This was before the age of large-scale urban excavations, but over Christmas and New Year 1965–66, Philip Barker and a group of dedicated volunteers were able to investigate an area of a few metres square. A massive Roman ditch, nearly 30 metres wide and over 6 metres deep, crossed the site and cut through Iron Age ditches and prehistoric occupation. The ditch and what remained of its internal rampart formed part of the Roman town defences. It was more than forty years before they would be investigated again (*see* Worcester castle).

The site was planned and the buildings designed by Shingler Risdon Associates. There is a varied palette of materials and forms, and most of the buildings are in scale with the streets around. However, the hotel tower dominates views of the cathedral from many angles, while the spiral ramps of the car park entrance in Friar Street seem a crude insult to the scale and character of Worcester's finest 'heritage' street.

The shopping centre was given a post-modern refacing in the late 1990s, mostly swept away in 2016–17 when a two-level food court was created facing the cathedral. The former Russell and Dorrell department store lives on through its art deco façades, successively dated 1925, 1932 and 1959, along the High Street.

Also within the shopping centre is St Andrew's Methodist Church on Pump Street (designed in 1966–67 by Norman Webster of Shingler Risdon Associates), replacing an Edwardian church. St Andrew's is on the second floor, its presence announced at street level by a spectacular full-height 'dalle de verre' (coloured glass set in concrete) window of abstract design, by Arthur Buss of Goddard & Gibbs.

The roundabout in front of the cathedral has now been replaced by a public square, providing a greatly improved setting both for the cathedral and for Ken Potts' Elgar statue. Beforehand, archaeological excavation of the centre of the old roundabout revealed some of the history of Lich Street, while former residents were interviewed for an oral history project.

5. Worcester Cathedral

Dominating the southern end of the High Street, Worcester Cathedral is by far the city's most prominent and best-known historic building. The see of Worcester covers Worcestershire and some outlying parishes, but originally extended as far south as Bristol. The cathedral tower can be seen from a large part of the diocese,

Worcester Cathedral across Cathedral Square.

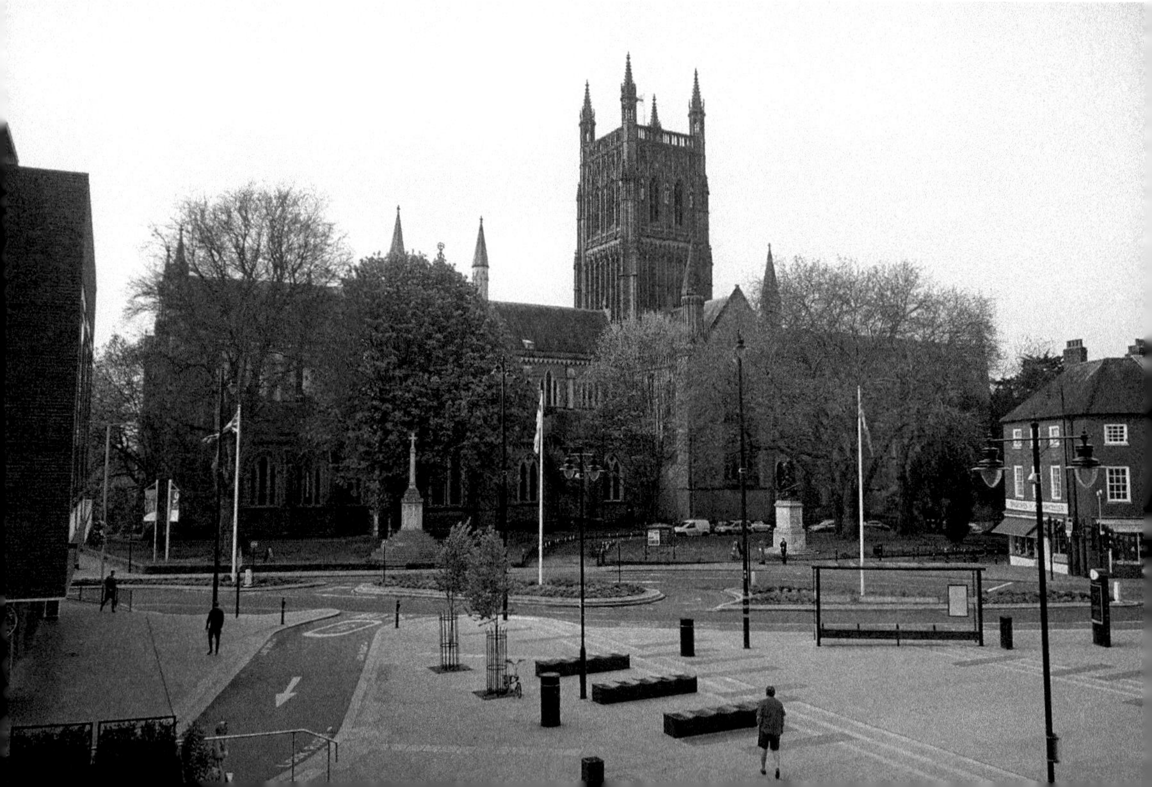

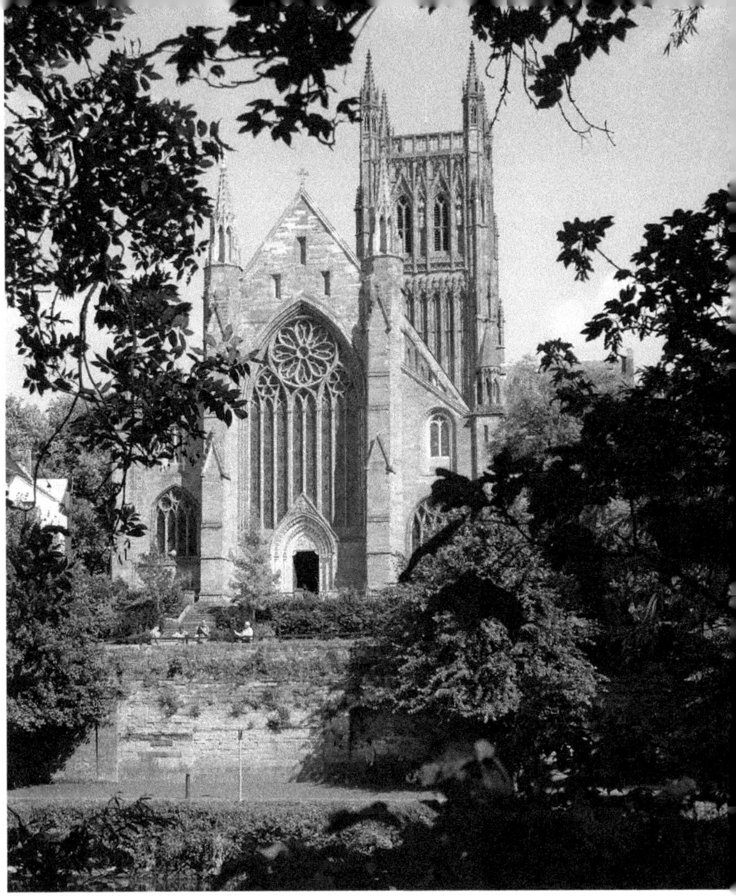

The west end of the cathedral from the river.

and one of the unexpected joys for visitors is the frequent appearance of the cathedral in views within the city.

Much of the cathedral's medieval history can only be clearly read inside. The most frequently used stone was new red sandstone from quarries at Holt and Ombersley, which has weathered very poorly. As a result, most of the building is faced with modern stone following multiple restorations in the nineteenth and twentieth centuries. The green sandstone, from Highley in Shropshire, is much finer. Both types of stone were brought down the Severn by boat.

The see was founded in 680, and Bishop Bosel's first cathedral church was dedicated to St Peter. Three hundred years later, in 983, Bishop Oswald added a second cathedral (dedicated to St Mary). The sites of both St Peter and St Mary are unknown, though probably below the medieval cathedral. Some reused columns with characteristic bulbous lathe-turned capitals, in the slype (now the café), are the most tangible remnants of one of the Anglo-Saxon buildings.

Bishop Wulfstan started to build a new cathedral in 1084, starting a programme of building and rebuilding that lasted, almost without a break, for some 300 years. The apse and twelve aisles of Wulfstan's crypt mark his cathedral's east end (the west end is still in the same place), and are the main early Norman survival. Later Norman masonry can be seen in the north and south transepts, remodelled around 1180–90, probably after the crossing tower fell in 1175. Norman stonework here is usually distinguished by a striped effect produced by the use of different coloured sandstones and limestone.

The two western bays of the nave, dating from a few years later, are a fine example of transitional style (late twelfth century), though incorporating earlier Norman masonry. They combine round and pointed arches, using paterae (circular mouldings) and chevron decoration to striking decorative effect. When the rest of the nave was rebuilt in the fourteenth century, these two bays were allowed to remain.

The Early English east end (choir, aisles, eastern transepts and Lady Chapel) is the result of a building campaign lasting from 1224 to around 1260, and is unified by a consistent use of tall Purbeck marble shafts to the pillars and windows. In many of the arch spandrels there are detailed carvings of biblical scenes and mythical monsters.

The richly ornamented and panelled crossing tower was rebuilt in 1357–74, and was the model for towers at Great Malvern and Gloucester Cathedral. It now houses the cathedral's bells, formerly in a free-standing tower on the north side, which were demolished after the Civil War.

Worcester Cathedral is home to two fine royal tombs. King John's is the oldest surviving English royal effigy, a noble figure carved from Purbeck marble. John died at Newark in 1216 but had asked to be buried at Worcester. His tomb was built fifteen years later and reconstructed in Tudor times. The bishops by his head are thought to be Oswald and Wulfstan. Close by is the chantry chapel of Prince Arthur. The heir to Henry VII, Arthur died at Ludlow Castle on his honeymoon, aged fifteen. The chapel is covered with heraldry including both the Tudor rose and the pomegranate of Granada, the emblem of his young widow, Catherine of Aragon (later Henry VIII's first wife), signifying the presence of not just English but European royalty.

A large set of medieval misericords is carved with Biblical scenes and illustrations of the Labours of the Months. Later furnishings include screens and choir stalls by Gilbert Scott. The cathedral library, housed in the space over the south aisle vault, has important collections including medieval music.

6. The Monastic Precinct, Worcester Cathedral

Contrasting with the open character of the north side of the cathedral, College Green, its buildings mostly Georgian or Victorian, retains the feel of an enclosed precinct, which was established when Bishop Oswald reformed Worcester into a Benedictine priory in 983, recreated after the return of the priory land from the castle in 1217. To either end there are contrasting fourteenth-century gatehouses: the Edgar Tower and the Watergate. To the south are remains of the stone precinct wall, while the riverside wall to the west incorporates remains of medieval buildings.

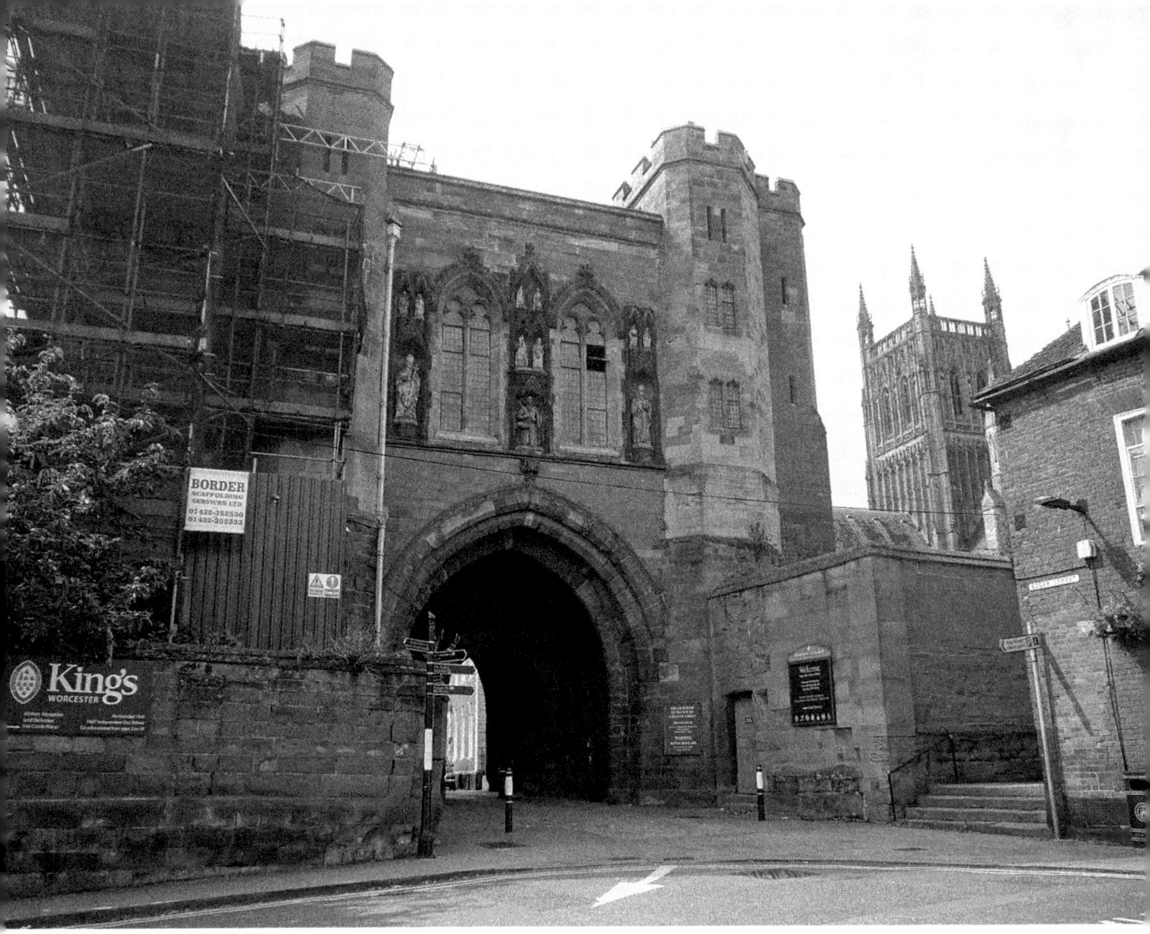

Above: Edgar Tower from Edgar Street.

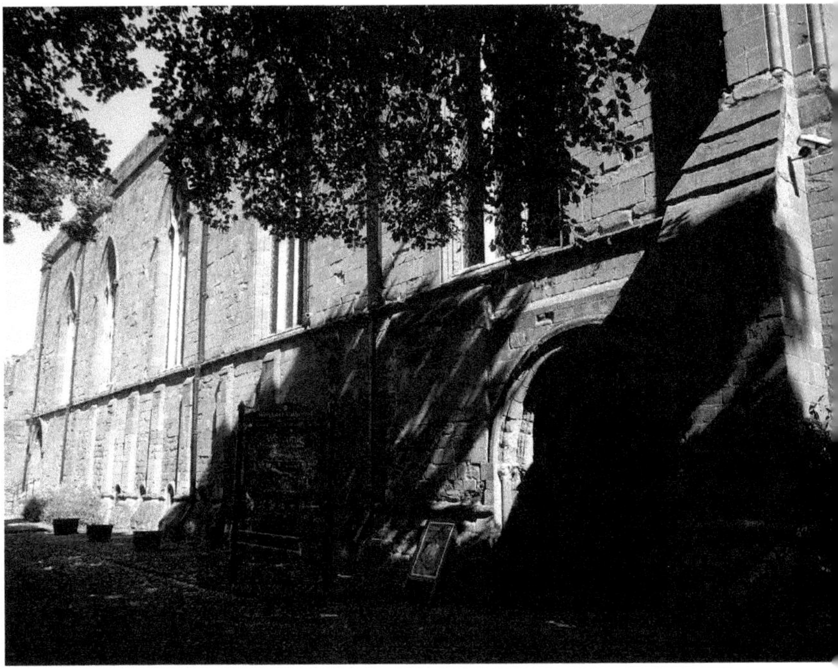

Right: The south side of College Hall.

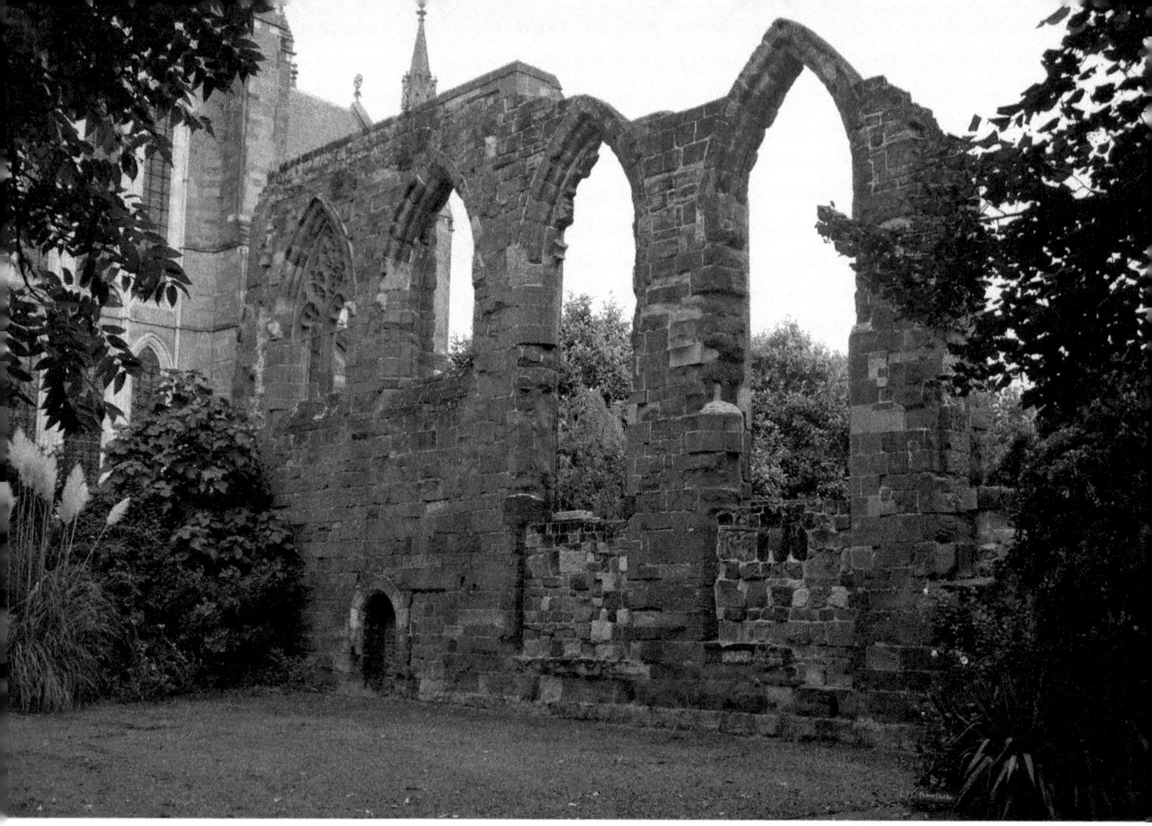

The Guesten Hall ruins.

The most extensive medieval survivals are around the cloister: the outer walls here are Norman, and the cloister walks were rebuilt in stages between the 1370s and 1430s. Opening off them are several earlier buildings including the chapter house and refectory. The fourteenth-century refectory (College Hall) has an early Norman undercroft. The carved stone Christ in Majesty on the east wall, dated to 1220–30, was retained from an earlier building. Although damaged when it was plastered over at the Reformation, it is a work of very high quality.

The chapter house of around 1100–20 is notable as the earliest 'centrally planned' example. It is circular inside, and originally outside too, though in the late fourteenth century the upper part and the outside were rebuilt to a decagonal plan. The central column dates to around 1240, but must replace an earlier column supporting a similar stone vault. The Norman stonework here is striped with Cotswold limestone and green Highley sandstone, and the bench seats against the walls retain traces of medieval painting. Archaeological excavation inside the chapter house revealed nearly 200 burials of men, women and children from Worcester's late Anglo-Saxon cemetery.

The Guesten Hall (built in 1320–40) stood east of the chapter house, but only one wall now survives. The remainder was demolished in 1862, and the magnificent timber roof was reused in the new church of Holy Trinity, Shrub Hill. When that too was demolished in the 1960s the roof was taken to Avoncroft Museum, where it now covers the New Guesten Hall. In a recent restoration cathedral stonemasons have had an opportunity to renew some of the intricate window tracery.

Towards the river are extensive undercrofts of the monastic reredorter and infirmary.

The mighty Edgar Tower, begun in 1346–47, and completed after 1368–69, forms an impressive entrance to the precinct from the city. Below the stone gatehouse is a cross wall with round-headed footway and carriageway openings and medieval wooden doors. The statues in niches on the façade date from a comprehensive Victorian restoration, and further restoration is underway in 2018.

The Watergate dates from 1378, and has a seventeenth-century house over the medieval archway. The medieval stonework has acquired much graffiti over the years, including the outline of a large fish of unknown date, perhaps a large salmon, or even a sturgeon.

On the north side of the cathedral the precinct has been dismembered. Both gateways (College Grates and Lich Gate) have gone, making way for road schemes in the 1790s and 1960s, respectively. The medieval city's cemetery occupied this side, along with the cemetery chapel (the Church of St Michael in Bedwardine), the site of which is now marked by a group of ledger slabs. Its Victorian replacement, also demolished, now lies under the road. Within the cemetery area are two county war memorials. The South African war memorial of 1908 has sculpted figures of a rifleman and a winged Victory by W. R. Colton. The First World War memorial, designed by R. Haughton, is a plain cross, modelled on the White Cross at Hereford.

7. Worcester Castle

In common with other major Midland towns (Hereford, Ludlow, Shrewsbury, Warwick), Worcester was provided with a powerful castle not long after the Norman Conquest. These castles were sited on the edge of town, as much to watch over the citizenry as to give them protection. While all the others have survived

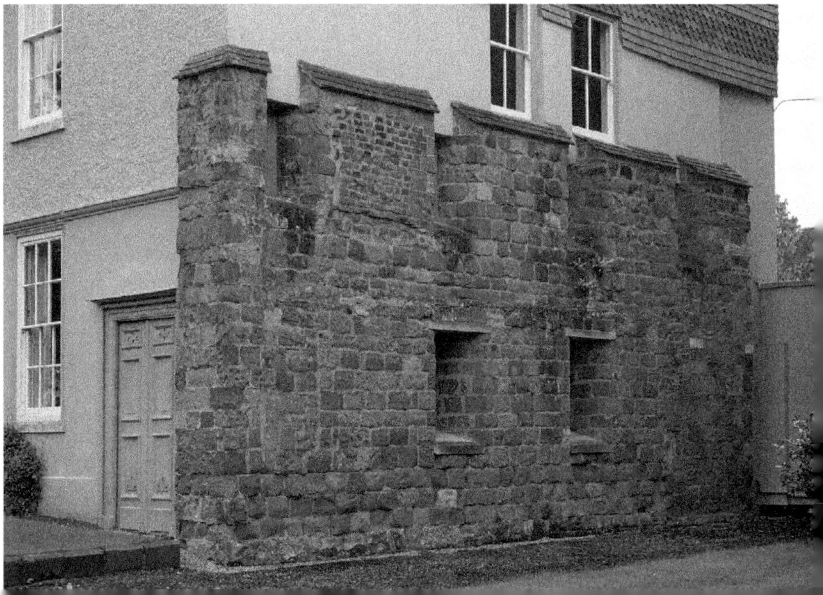

The chamber block wall, Worcester Castle.

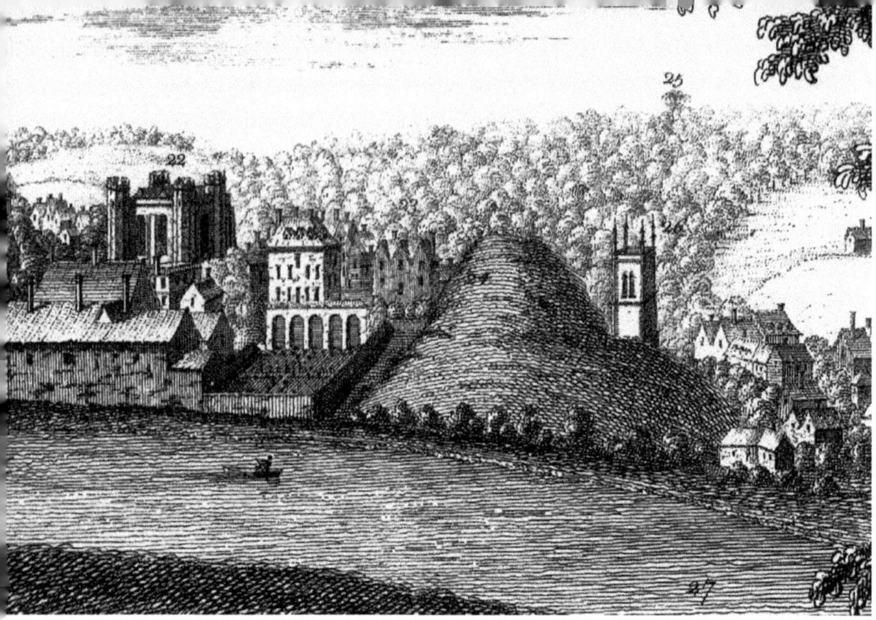

The castle motte as engraved by Samuel and Nathaniel Buck in 1732.

to a greater or lesser extent, Worcester's castle has become all but invisible. The reasons for this lie in its medieval history.

In 1069, Urse d'Abitot, Norman sheriff of Worcestershire, appropriated priory land to build his castle at the southern end of the city. This was very unpopular at the time (Ealdred, Archbishop of York and former Bishop of Worcester wrote: 'Hightest thou Urse? Have thou God's curse'), and was not forgotten. In 1217 the young Henry III returned a large part, though not all, of this land to the priory, which is thought to have been a dying wish of his father John. The castle was already in decline, and losing this land rendered it useless militarily. The remnant continued in use mainly as a prison, and as a Bridewell this use continued until 1814.

The most visible surviving fragment of Worcester Castle is a stone wall incorporated into Castle House on College Green. This two-storey wall is dated to the late twelfth century from the string-course mouldings and small windows. The architectural details on the outside wall of the medieval building are now inside Castle House, and what can be seen outside was the inner wall face. The building seems to have been around 24 metres long and 9 metres wide and has a domestic appearance. Stylistically it appears to date to around 1170–90. It was probably a chamber block, and quite likely the 'King's chamber', on which work was done in 1192 (expenditure on the castle is also recorded in 1172–73). Another probable survivor is a stone arcade, which forms part of the Deanery, just to the west.

Severn Street follows the outer edge of the castle ditch (now buried). The earthen motte stood on the King's School site until the 1820s–30s, when it was levelled and the materials sold. Many Roman artefacts were recovered and formed an early part of the Worcester City Museum collection; these were probably from the town's cemetery.

As well as forming an important part of Worcester's medieval history, the castle provides evidence of the continuity of the settlement from its earliest origins. Excavation of part of the bailey rampart before the construction of the Keyes

Building revealed it to have origins in the early Iron Age. Radiocarbon dates of the eight to fourth centuries BC show that the earthwork had its origins a full one and a half millennia before the castle. It had served as part of Worcester's defence through the Iron Age, the Roman and Anglo-Saxon periods before finding a new use as part of the castle.

8. Michael Baker Boathouse (King's School)

King's School's new boathouse, opened in 2012, is named for the donor, a former pupil. It is an elegant and effective response to an awkward site. The long narrow plot, previously occupied by an ugly 1950s concrete boathouse, is constrained by walls and a road, and was once part of the castle ditch. The design, by Associated Architects (who also designed the school's Keyes Building, further up Severn Street), has drawn on both the boat form and materials used in boatbuilding.

The building does much more than merely house rowing boats, providing a workshop, training and changing areas, and teaching and reception space. Energy efficiency has been built in throughout. The ground floor (the boathouse itself) is built in carefully bonded brown brick, laid in variants of English and

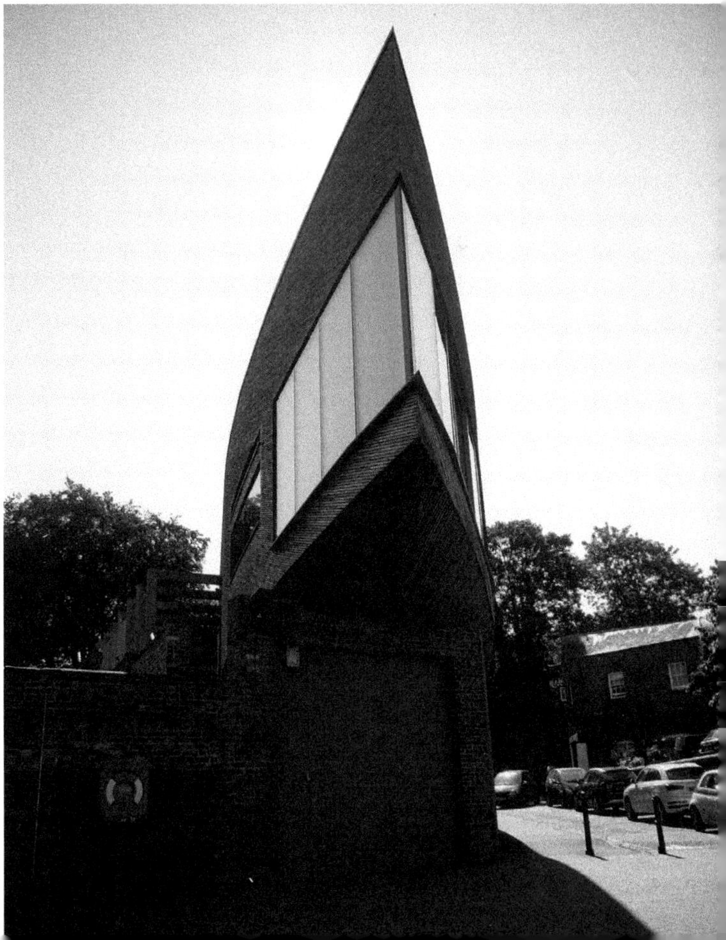

The prow of the King's School boathouse.

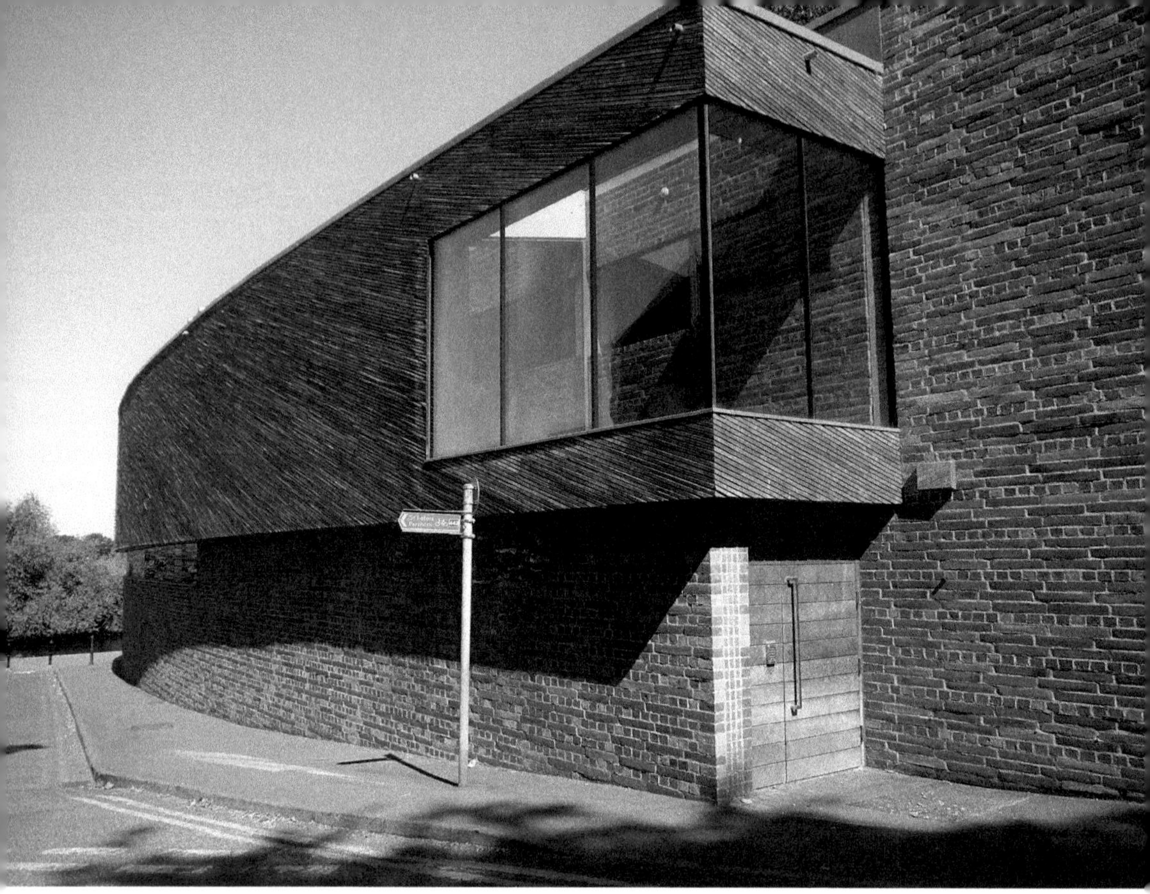

Side view of King's School boathouse.

English garden wall bonds, using unusual specially made double-length stretchers. The contrasting upper floor is faced with narrow diagonal strips of chestnut. The first-floor prow of the 'boat' is cantilevered out over the footpath towards the river, providing a dramatic new landmark for Worcester's riverside, and it is glazed on both sides to allow views through to the cathedral beyond.

9. Royal Worcester Porcelain, Severn Street

Worcester was home to one of Britain's largest and most enduring porcelain companies, and also the largest concentration of porcelain works outside the Potteries. The name of Royal Worcester lives on, though manufacture now takes place abroad and there is no remaining presence in Worcester itself. Its heritage survives in the fine porcelain vessels, statues and other products made here, examples of which can be seen in the Museum of Royal Worcester next door, and also in a series of buildings that illustrate its history through the nineteenth and twentieth centuries.

The history of porcelain manufacturing is characterised by technical and design change and business uncertainty, and many companies were very short-lived.

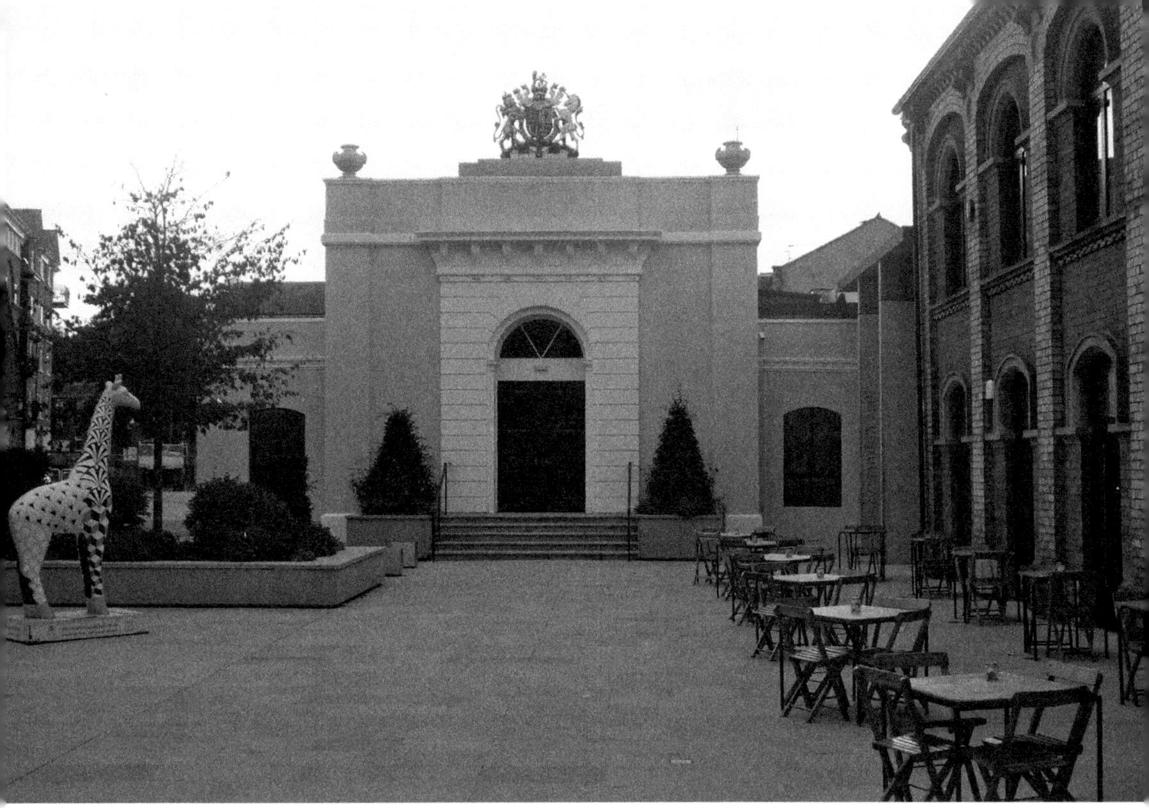

Above: Royal Worcester's 1852 showroom, now the Henry Sandon Hall.

Below: Scrivener and Sutton's buildings along Severn Street.

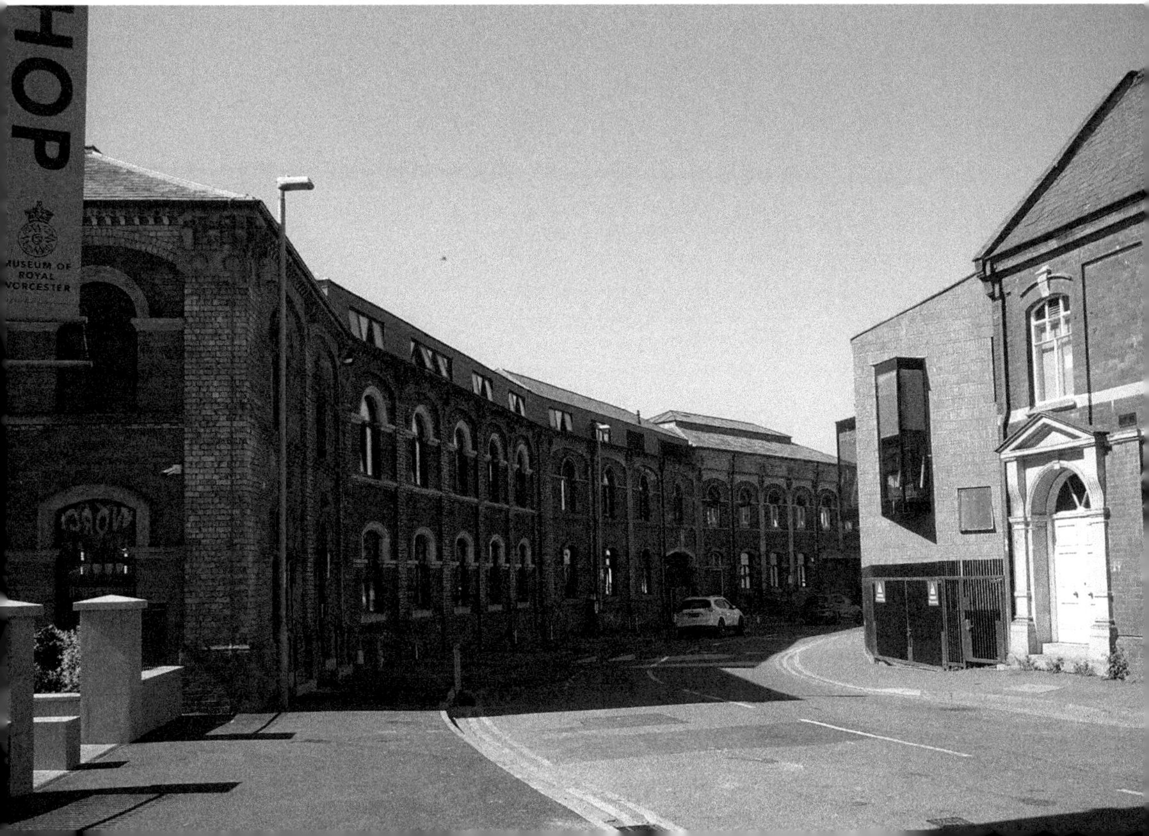

Worcester's lifespan from 1751 to 2008 is exceptional. The earliest manufacture took place on the riverside at Warmstry Slip. Robert Chamberlain set up business in 1783 on the opposite side of the city, in Severn Street, initially as a decorator rather than a potter. With the foundation of Grainger's in the early nineteenth century, there were three rival enterprises in Worcester. Chamberlain's and the Flight, Barr & Barr Company came together in 1840 on this site

The merged company embarked on a major building campaign in 1852; all buildings earlier than this have since been swept away. The architect chosen to extend the factory was Robert Armstrong, a specialist in porcelain works. His buildings are laid out as fingers radiating from the factory core towards the Worcester & Birmingham Canal. Later buildings include Scrivener's (1865) and Sutton's (1887–91) curving façades along Severn Street, which drew on designs for a model factory in the Arboretum.

Porcelain works had to accommodate the dirtiest of processes, such as the preparation of clay and slip, alongside the delicate work of finishing and decorating, requiring spotlessly clean surroundings. Typically the buildings were long, narrow and tall to allow as much natural light through large windows on both sides. Armstrong's Pan Grinding House, with its truncated chimney, is the best preserved of the historic buildings, retaining much of the original Victorian machinery and pans for grinding colours and other materials. Unfortunately this has made it hard to find a suitable use and it remains empty. The former showroom has recently been converted into the Henry Sandon Hall. Most of the other buildings have either been converted to residential use or demolished. Royal Worcester themselves were ruthless in removing redundant buildings, or radically altering them for new uses.

During the Second World War the works were turned over to the production of spark plugs. This period is recalled by the survival of an air-raid watcher's post on top of the new workshops building, capping off the gap left by the removal of a large factory chimney.

10. The Commandery

The Commandery is well known for its Civil War associations, but the buildings tell a fascinating series of very different stories spanning 800 years, and probably longer. It is just outside the medieval walls. As a private house, it survived Civil War destruction because it was within the defensive lines linking to Fort Royal, which contained the Sidbury suburb.

The dedication of the Commandery chapel to St Gudwal (or Godwald), a little-known Welsh bishop, suggests that it may have originated in the Anglo-Saxon period. Bishop Oswald of Worcester (961–92) had spent time at the monastery of Blandinberg (Ghent), where Gudwal's relics were kept, and it is plausible that he founded a chapel here in the late tenth century.

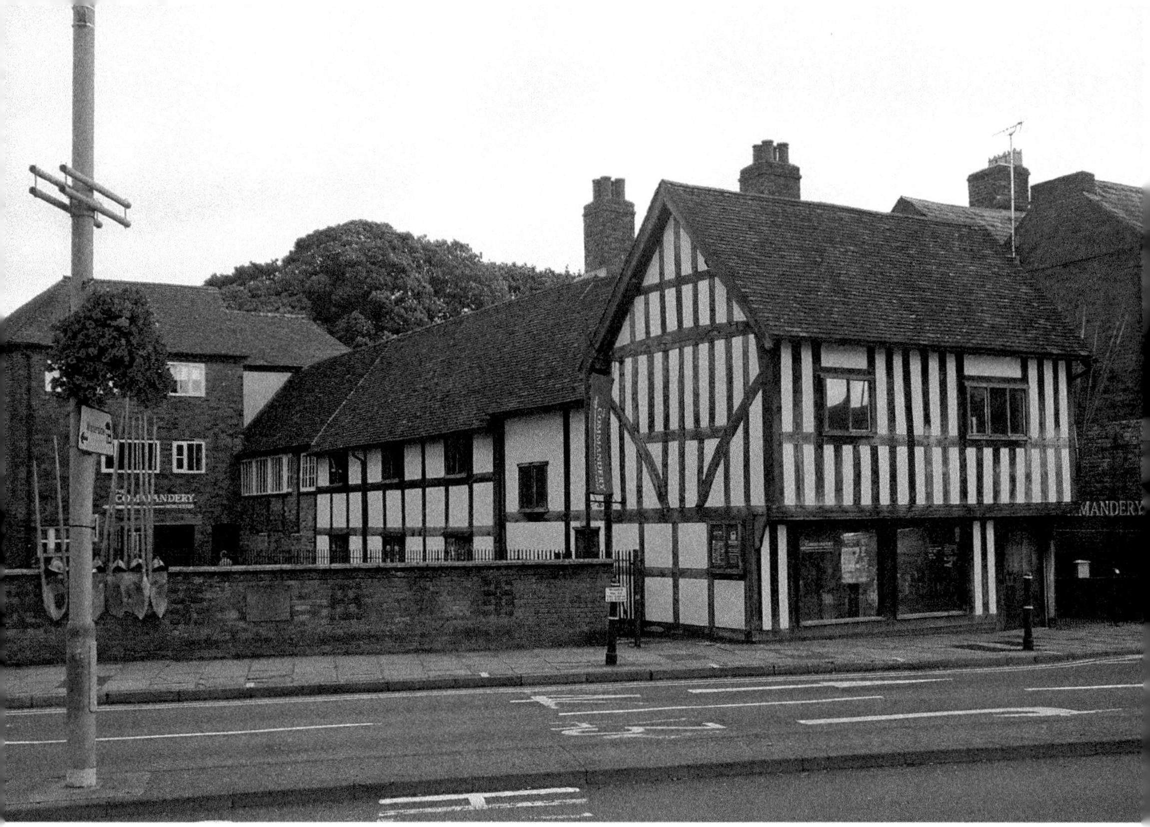

Above: View of the Commandery across Sidbury Bridge, site of the medieval city ditch.

Below: Excavated east end of the Commandery chapel.

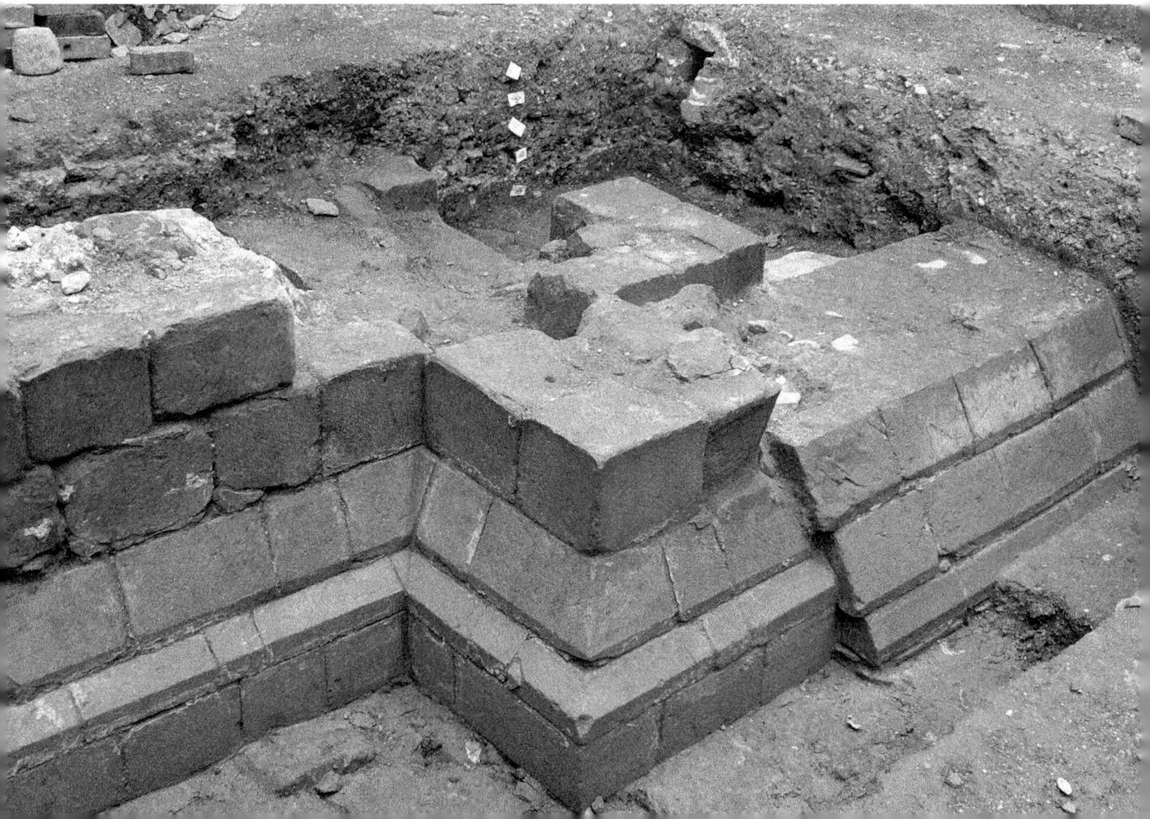

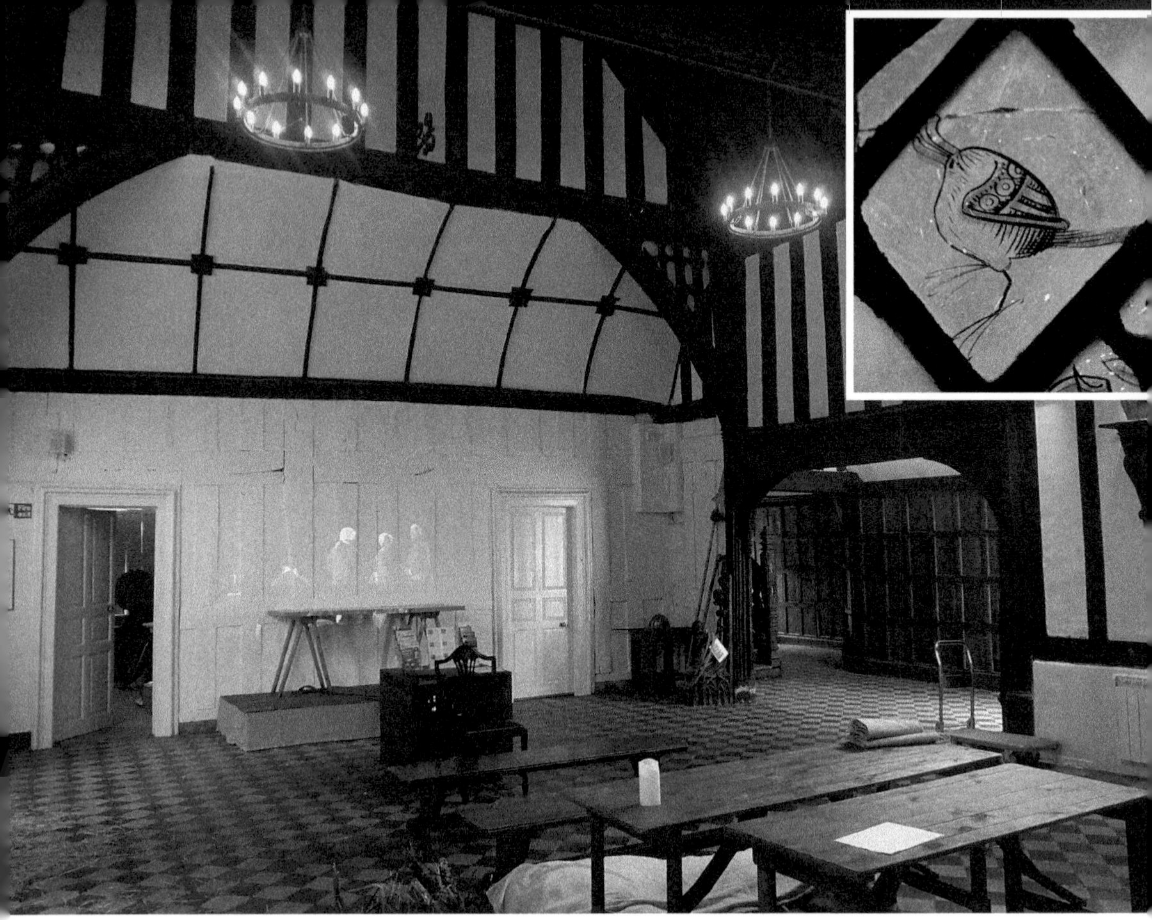

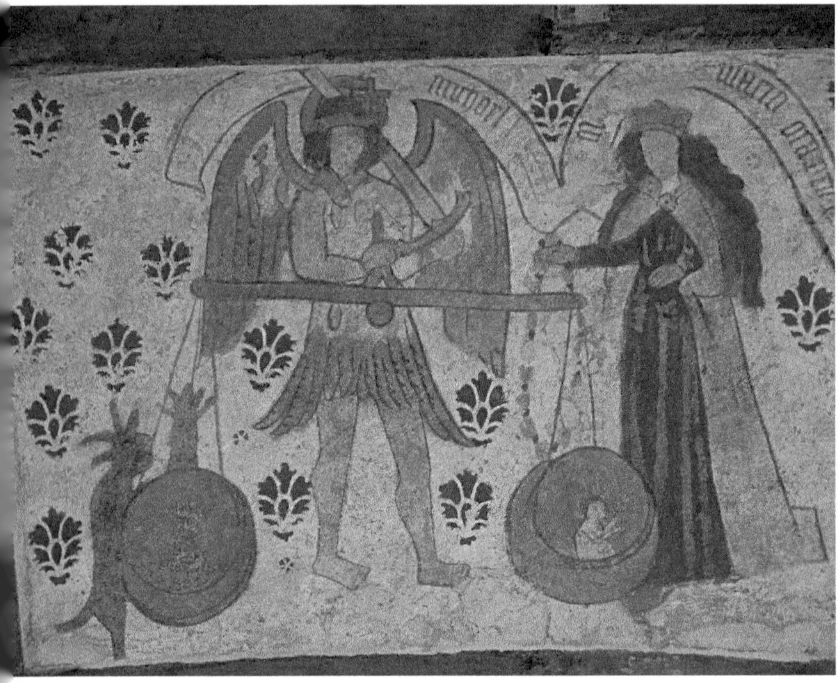

Above: The Great Hall.

Inset: Stained glass in the Great Hall bay window.

Left: Wall painting of St Michael weighing souls at the Last Judgement.

The origins of the Commandery itself were as a medieval hospital dedicated to St Wulfstan and run by Augustinian canons. The earliest record is in 1221, when Thomas of Eldersfield, who had been blinded and castrated after losing a judicial duel, was miraculously restored after being cared for here. The institution was mainly home to wealthy elderly people, known as 'corrodians', who signed over their possessions to the hospital.

The earlier medieval plan, partially revealed by excavation in 2005–06, seems to have been quite haphazard. The buildings were probably timber framed on stone foundations. The exception was the thirteenth-century chapel, whose east end was found. Built in green Highley sandstone, this was a small building of high quality. Forty-nine masons' marks were found on the stonework, several of which can be matched with marks at the cathedral, suggesting that the cathedral masons may have worked here. Angle buttresses marked the east end of the chancel, and a north chapel was added in the fifteenth century. Both were demolished in the sixteenth century, making way for new domestic accommodation.

In the late 1470s all of the buildings apart from the chapel were swept away, to be replaced by timber-framed buildings around two courtyards, linked by the Great Hall or refectory. Tree-ring dating has established that timbers for the buildings were felled in 1468–73, and construction would have followed a year or two later.

The medieval buildings include the close-studded timber-framed Great Hall, with an ornate hammer-beam roof (later converted to tie beam), with wind braces and carved bosses. It has a fine bay window with medieval stained glass, a cross passage and the seventeenth-century west gallery. The Great Hall was damaged in 1843 when a carriageway was driven through, and this was only undone in 1954.

The east wing was the master's accommodation and included a first-floor solar, again with an elaborately decorated roof. The blocked doorway visible at first-floor level within the courtyard probably led onto a staircase leading to the chapel.

In 1467, the city had adopted Ordinances, which included an early form of building regulations. These aimed to protect the important tiling industry, requiring that new buildings should have tiled rather than thatched roofs, and that the tilers should mark their products. Medieval tiles with stamped tilemakers' marks, probably made between 1467 and around 1525, have only been found in and around Worcester. Over 200 stamped tiles have been found on the roofs of the Commandery, with over thirty different stamps representing either workshops or individual tilers.

The wall paintings of around 1490 in the west wing were rediscovered in the 1930s and restored by Elsie Matley Moore. They were restored again by Perry Lithgow in 2006–07. They include depictions of the martyrdom of St Erasmus – his death, whereby his intestines were wound out on a windlass, has made him the patron saint of sufferers of intestinal pains as well as women in labour – and St Gudwal.

When the monastic institution was dissolved in 1540, the Commandery was bought by the Wylde family, and it remained a private house until the late nineteenth century. In 1651 it served as a Royalist headquarters, and the Duke of Hamilton died here from injuries suffered in the Battle of Worcester. Later, an east-facing garden front was created by encasing the medieval timber frame in brick and adding a new wing to the north-east (tree-ring dated to around 1708).

From 1866 to 1887 the Commandery housed Worcester's first school for blind people, and the first for blind adults anywhere (the College for the Blind Sons of Gentlemen). F. T. Marsh, who published the first history of the Commandery in 1890, studied here. Following this, Littlebury's printers occupied the buildings. In 1973, on the closure of Littlebury's, the Commandery was purchased by Worcester City Council and restored as a museum, focusing on the Civil War. It is now one of the main sites of Museums Worcestershire.

11. Sidbury Gate and the City Walls

Worcester's city walls survive at many places along their medieval circuit of over a mile and a half. This was probably marked from the late 1100s by a rampart, palisade and ditch, with substantial constructions only at the entry points, where gatehouses and bridges were built. Murage grants (taxes raised to build

Sidbury Gate as discovered in 1907. (Berrow's Worcester Journal)

Inset: Sidbury Gate in the eigheenth century. (The 1769 edition of the Battle of Worcester map)

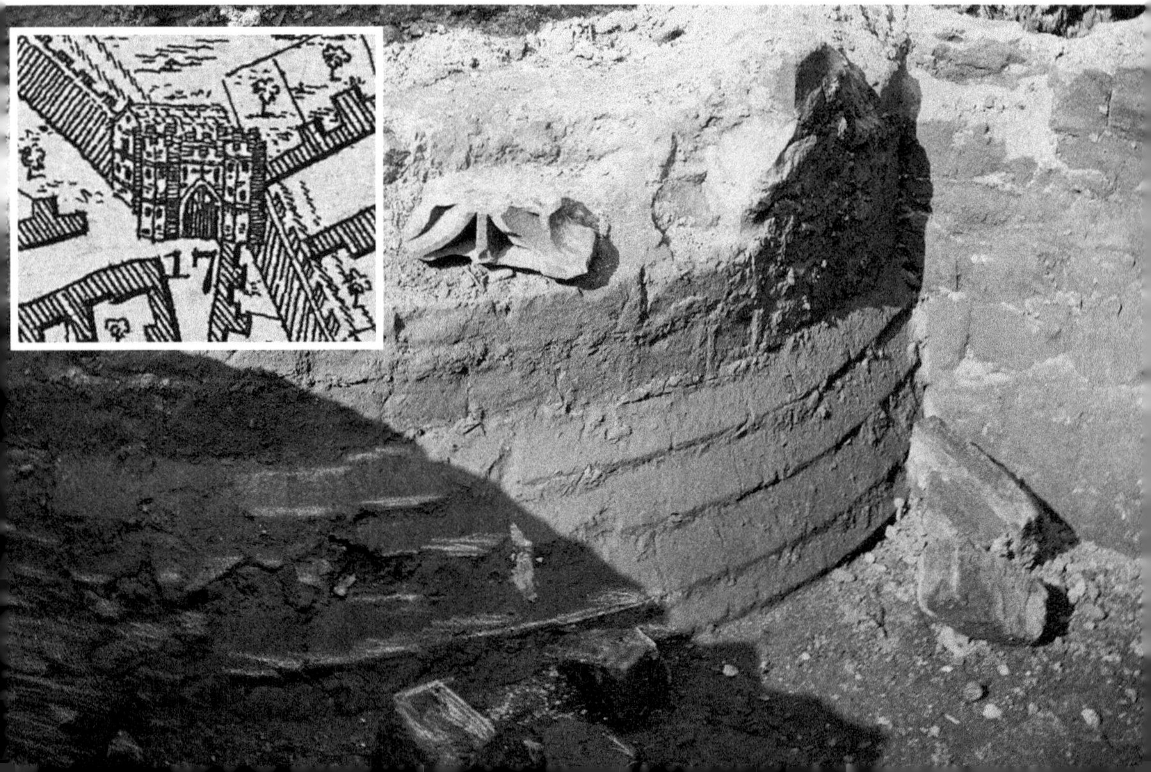

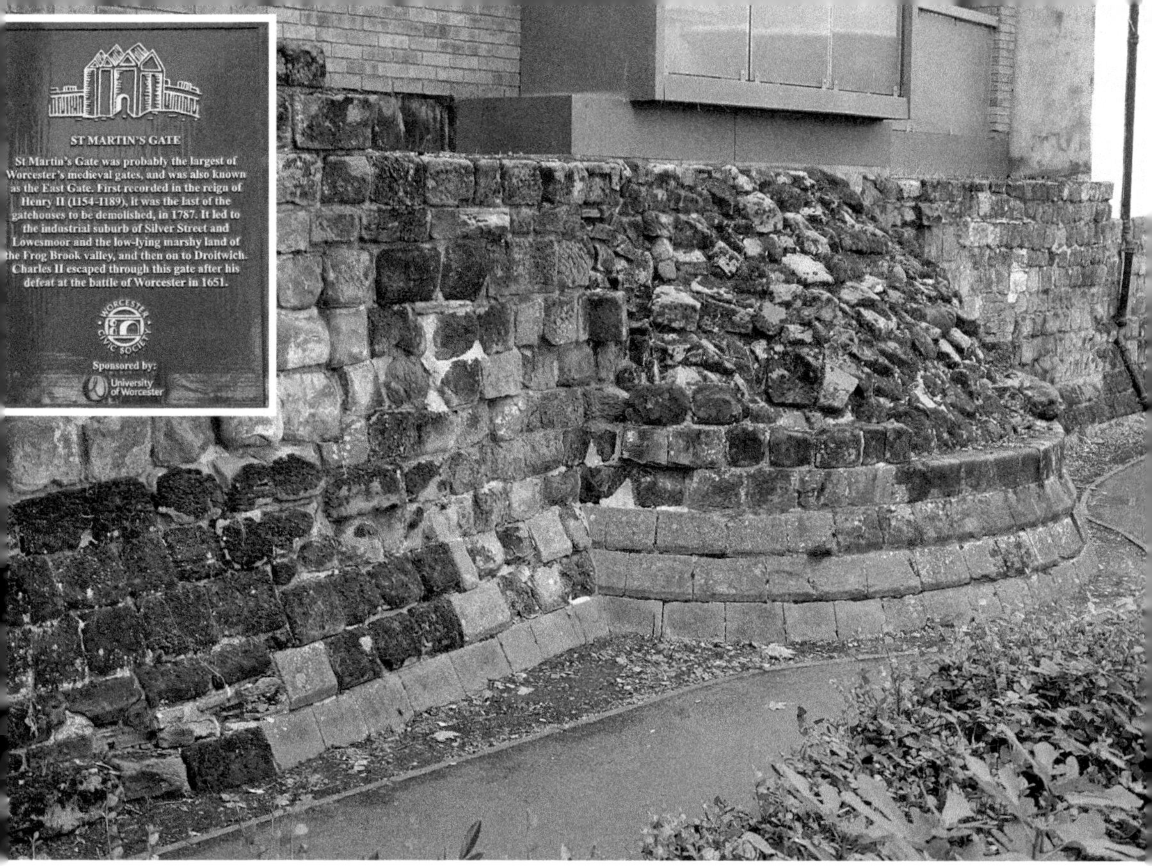

A bastion on the city walls revealed during clearance for City Walls Road in the 1970s.

Inset: Plaque marking the site of St Martin's Gate.

or maintain the walls) are recorded between 1224 and 1439, and stone walls eventually replaced the timber defences.

Worcester had been attacked several times in the twelfth century, and the walls seem to have deterred further attacks. On his way to fight at Evesham in 1265, Prince Edward (the future Edward I) avoided Worcester and crossed the Severn at Northwick. Crucially, having walls and gates meant better security for the merchants of the city, as well as allowing taxes to be collected by the city authorities, while the gates were locked at night to keep 'undesirables' out.

The only time that the medieval walls saw serious action was during the Civil War (1642–51). For at least a century before this the walls were in poor repair, and the advent of artillery meant significant replanning. Earth ramparts were added inside and outside the walls, with additional fortifications including artillery bastions. A fort was built at Fort Royal, overlooking the city, to deny this commanding height to any attackers. These preparations were not wasted. Worcester was briefly besieged in 1643, and again for two months in 1646, when the Parliamentary army built a ring of forts to encircle the city, eventually forcing its surrender. Again in 1651 the defences were brought back into use as the Royalists prepared to meet Cromwell in battle. Afterwards, Parliament ordered the slighting (destruction) of the walls. Within half a century they had been abandoned and the land was being sold for development.

Until the late 1960s very little of the walls could be seen. Several stretches of wall were rediscovered during clearance for City Walls Road, though some well-preserved parts were destroyed. None of the eight gatehouses survives above ground, as all were demolished between 1700 and 1787 to ease traffic flow; when Valentine Green was writing in 1764, only Sidbury and St Martin's were still standing. A public subscription was raised for the demolition of Sidbury Gate, on the main road to London, as the City Corporation would not allocate the funds.

Sidbury Gate was one of the four main gatehouses on the medieval circuit (the others were St Martins, Foregate and Bridge Gate), and is the only one where substantial remains survive. Following its demolition in 1769, it was unseen until a new shop was built on the site in 1907. Excavation for the cellar revealed part of the city wall, and the lower part of a massive circular gate tower with its chamfered plinth, and these were preserved during construction. They were later forgotten, however, and it was only in 1998 that new owners discovered an unexpected cellar, along with the remains of Sidbury Gate.

Sidbury Gate played an important role in the Battle of Worcester, as it was here that the Scots of the Royalist army held the Parliamentarians for just long enough to allow Charles II to escape the city following the fall of Fort Royal.

Other parts of the walls can be seen along City Walls Road, including a semicircular bastion, and in The Butts, near the Hive. The gatehouse sites have been marked with plaques erected by Worcester Civic Society.

12. Fownes Hotel, City Walls Road

Worcester's largest glove factory closed in 1973 and stood empty for over a decade until the buildings were converted into the Fownes Hotel in 1985. The factory was designed in stages by the prolific local architects Yeates and Jones (1882–83), for the Fownes company, who relocated from London. The three-storey red and blue brick building extends to twenty-seven bays and has a central pediment with a clock. In front, the City Walls Road dual carriageway sweeps past one of very few legacies of the 1948 Minoprio and Spencely plan for Worcester.

Glove making was a natural byproduct of the region's rich farming heritage. Leather for gloves was treated in Worcester's many tanneries, mostly sited close to the banks of the Severn, or along streams, where there was a ready source of water and an outlet for the noxious effluents.

At the height of the industry, in the decades either side of 1800, there were over 150 glove works in Worcester, employing over 30,000 people in and around the city. By 1830 consolidation had reduced the number to 108, and by the 1880s

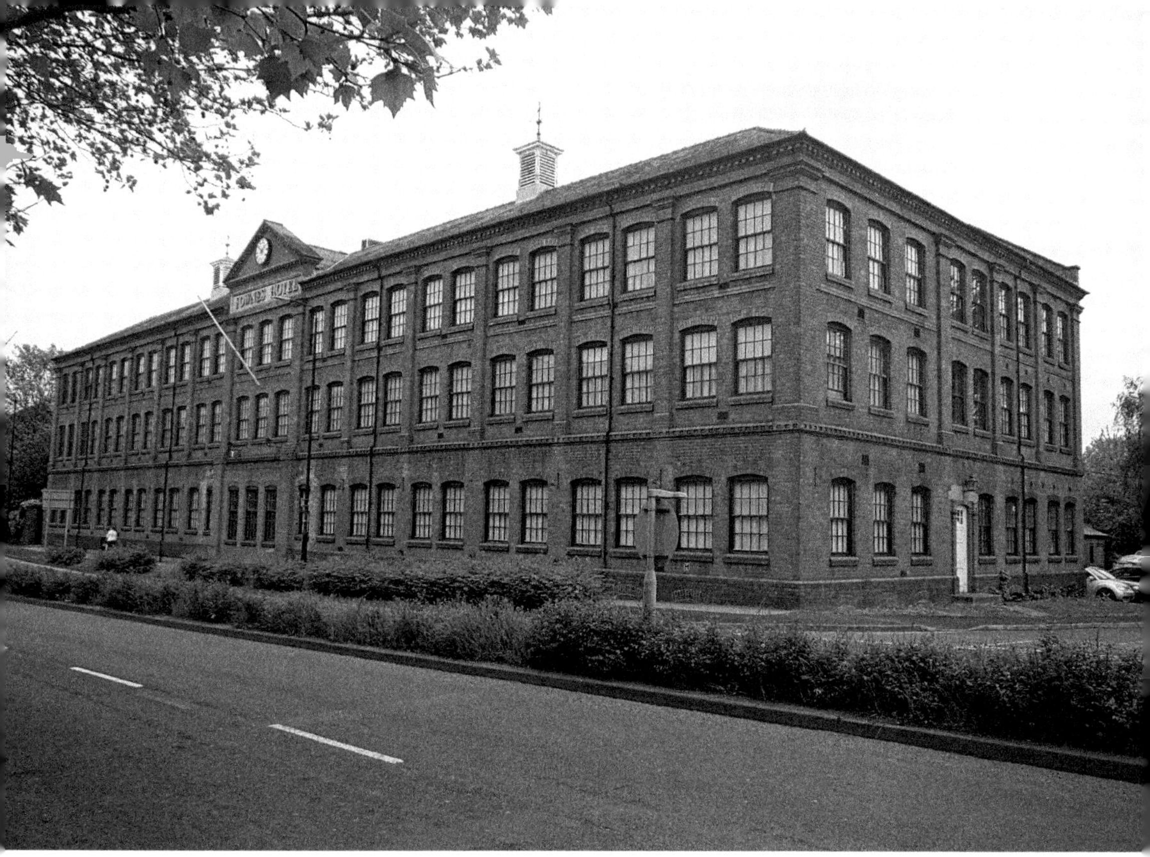

The main façade of the former Fownes glove factory.

there were just eleven. Most early glove works were small, and the Fownes factory in Talbot Street was almost the only one on a truly 'industrial' scale.

There are now no glove makers working in Worcester. Fownes Brothers is still a major international glove maker, now based in the United States and manufacturing in the Philippines and China.

13. Tudor House, Friar Street

Tudor House Museum is housed in a group of late sixteenth-century buildings on the west side of Friar Street. Originally domestic, with weavers' workshops behind, later uses included the Cross Keys pub. In the early twentieth century Richard Cadbury restored the building for use as the Tudor Coffee House. Since the 1970s Tudor House has been a local history museum. Formerly part of Worcester City Museums, it is now run by a community group, the Worcester Heritage and Amenity Trust.

The four-bay façade displays close-studded timber framing to the upper floor, which is jettied, while the ground floor is largely occupied by shopfronts. The jetty undulates gently along the length of the building, as the frame has settled over the years. The first-floor casement windows replace earlier oriels.

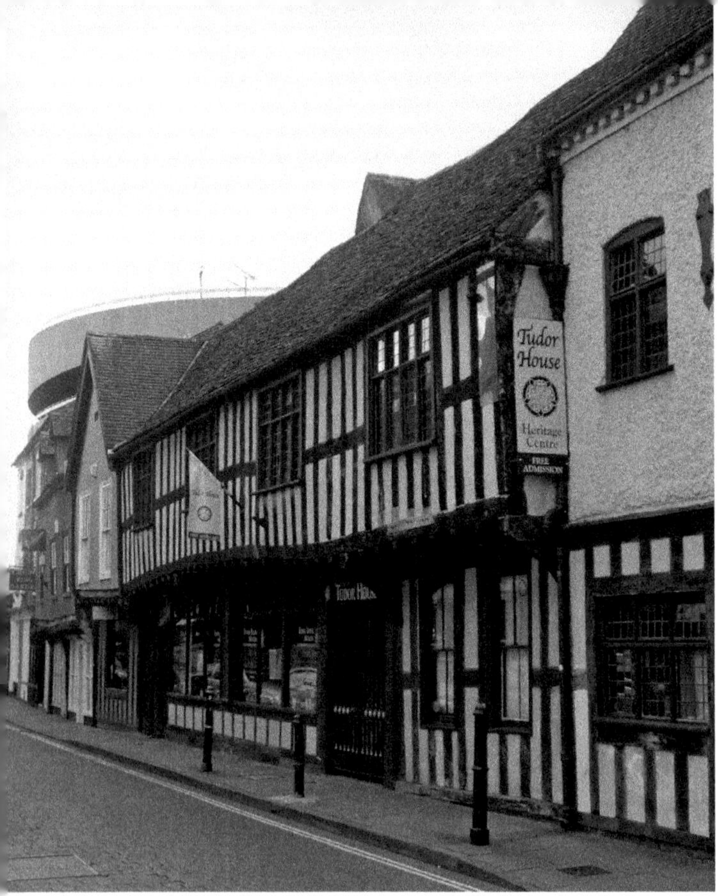

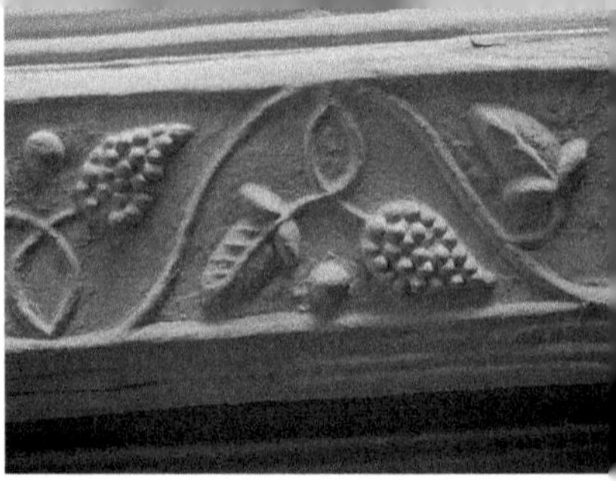

Above: Detail of the plaster ceiling.

Left: Tudor House on Friar Street.

Inside there are three large stone-built open fireplaces. The finest feature is an early seventeenth-century moulded plaster ceiling on the first floor. Curved plaster ribs enclose lions, prancing horses, fleurs-de-lis and rosettes, while the central timber beam is decorated with a vine scroll.

14. The Greyfriars, Friar Street

The Greyfriars is Worcester's finest medieval house. It was not connected in any way to the Greyfriars friary, which stood next door. Rather it was a very large private house, with a street frontage 4 perches (20 metres) wide, built for Thomas Grene, a brewer, one of the city's wealthiest citizens, and High Bailiff of Worcester in 1493–97.

Grene's initials, and those of his wife Elizabeth, are carved prominently on shields either side of the arched carriage entrance. The three-storey façade has close-studded timber framing, and is richly decorated, with a heavily moulded bressumer beam to the first-floor jetty and carved bargeboards on the two street-facing gables. In 2017 tree-ring cores were taken from some of the original timbers. These precisely dated the felling of the trees to 1489, so the house was probably built in 1490.

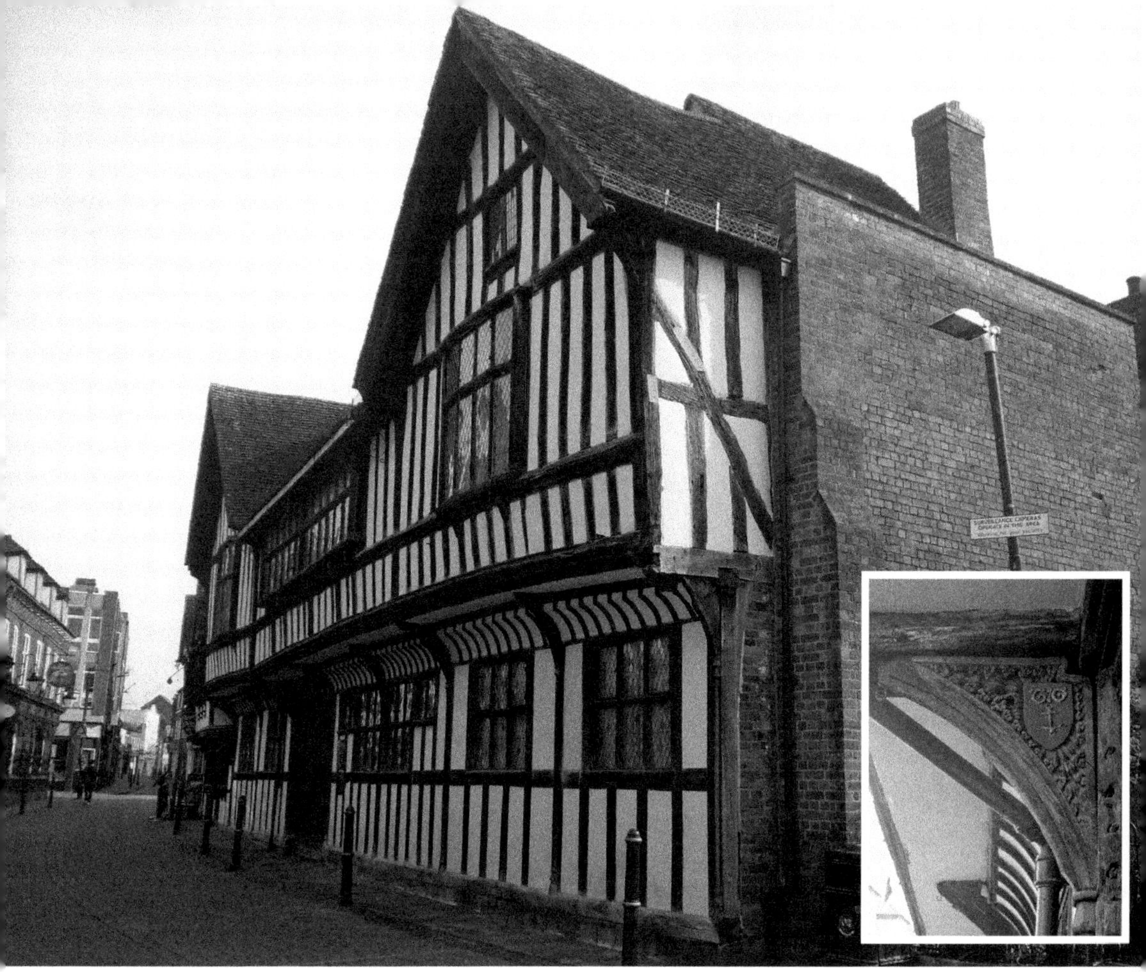

The Greyfriars.

Inset: Shield with the initials of Thomas Grene.

Over a century after Grene, the house was still a high-status residence, having passed through many hands. Modernisation for the Street family in the early seventeenth century included the large first-floor oriel (the second-floor oriels are early twentieth century, though may reflect the earlier arrangements), and new rear wings.

In the eighteenth century the house was subdivided, and in the nineteenth century became a pub (the Old Oak Inn) and shops – shopfronts were inserted along the full length of the façade. Behind the medieval house, twelve houses were packed into Court No. 6, Friar Street (or Georges Yard), one of sixteen numbered residential courts in Friar Street. In 1881, nine of the forty residents of Georges Yard worked in the gloving industry. As late as 1911, what are now tranquil gardens were home to fifty-six people. This is a pattern that would have been repeated all over the city centre.

The interior of the house contains fireplaces and moulded beams of the fifteenth century, timber carvings added by the Streets in the seventeenth century, and panelling and other features brought here from other houses in the twentieth century.

The Greyfriars found itself under threat of demolition in the mid-twentieth century. It was rescued by the Worcestershire Archaeological Society and by Matley Moore and his sister Elsie. The Moores lived in and restored the house, removing the shopfronts and other later changes, demolishing Georges Yard and creating a garden, and reinstating much of the medieval character. They lived here for thirty years. In 1966 the Greyfriars was given to the National Trust, together with the fifteenth-century houses opposite.

15. Nash House, New Street

Formerly called Glover Street, New Street is by no means new, containing several of Worcester's oldest buildings. At four storeys, Nash House is the tallest timber-framed building in Worcester. Each storey is jettied, and the three street-facing gables lean out gently over the road. As with other buildings of this date and status, the use of large quantities of timber in the close studding of the façade makes a conspicuous statement of wealth. To the rear is more conventional, and less expensive, square timber framing.

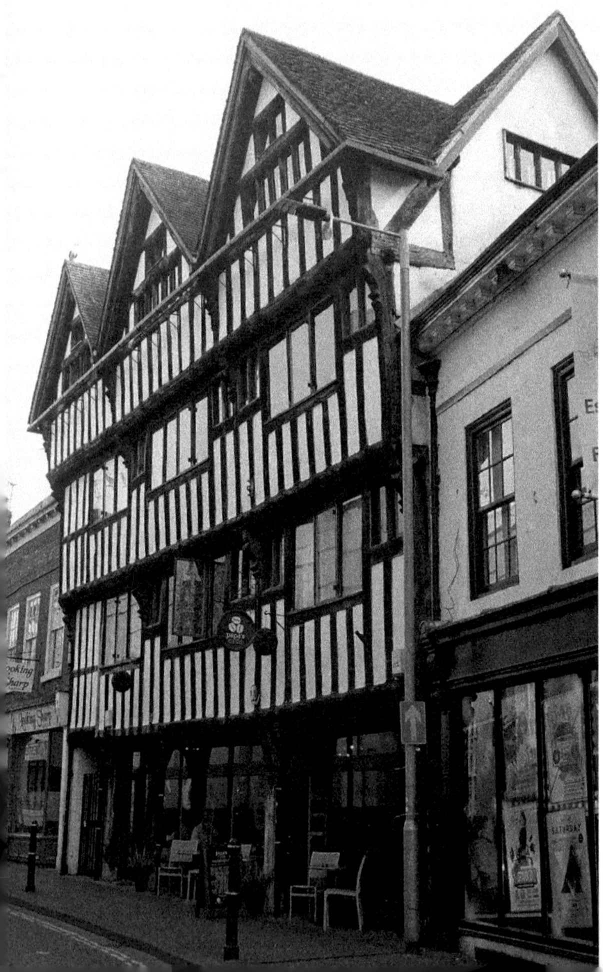

The New Street façade of Nash House.

The house was built for the Nash family, and timber to build it had been cut and was lying in Warndon Wood in 1605 when Richard Nash died, leaving it to his son, the city alderman John Nash, to build the house. Later additions by members of the family included the diamond brick chimney stacks and a coach access.

Nash House was restored by Henry Gorst in 1966, when buildings to the rear, including a rumoured (but rather unlikely) timber-framed shot tower, were demolished. The glazed ground floor (after removal of Victorian shopfronts) now houses a coffee shop, and the upper floors have been divided into flats.

16. King Charles House, Cornmarket and New Street

Originally one of Worcester's largest timber-framed houses, King Charles House faces both New Street and Cornmarket. Charles II lodged here in August 1651, and it was from here on the evening of 3 September that he slipped, disguised, when the battle was lost, to begin his epic escape to France.

As it was built in the sixteenth century, the house was two storeyed; the jettied upper storey with four gables was added in the seventeenth century. The main

King Charles House in Cornmarket and New Street.

Inset: Timber inscription, originally on the porch of King Charles House.

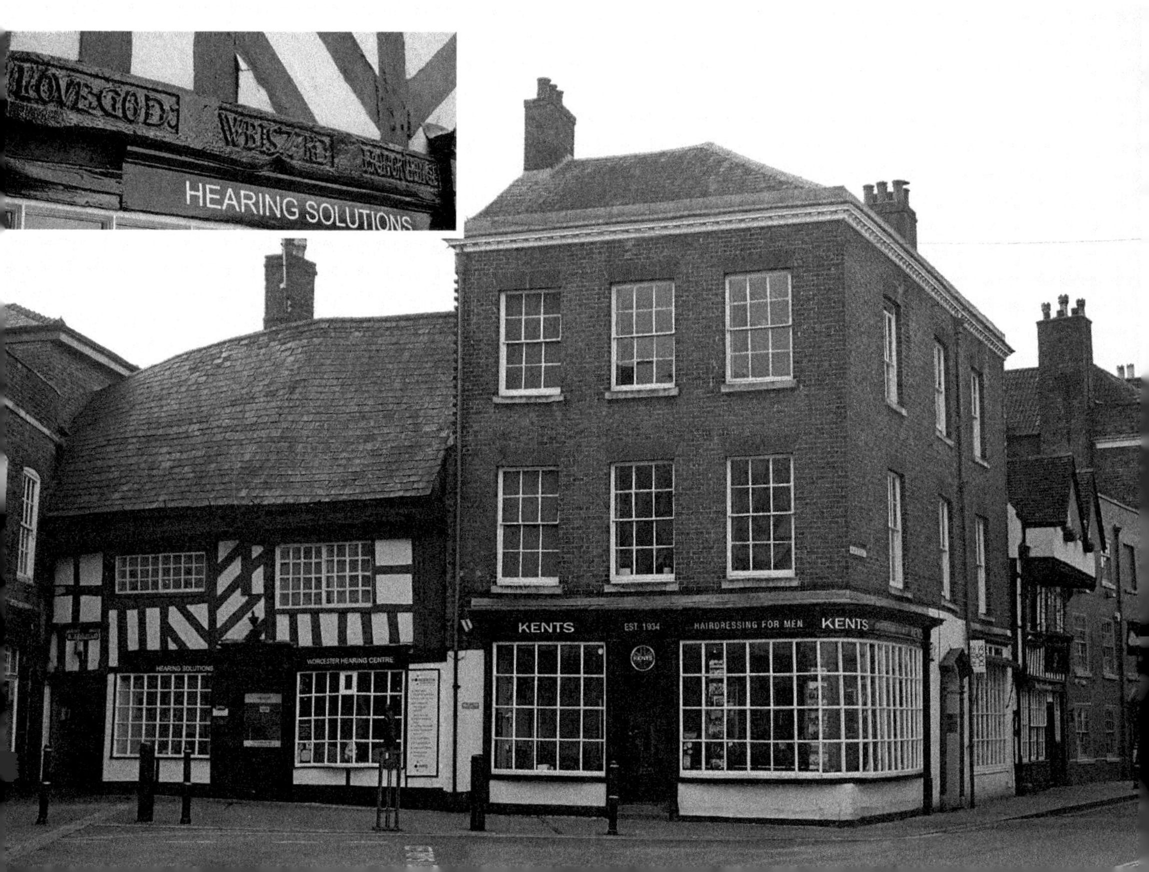

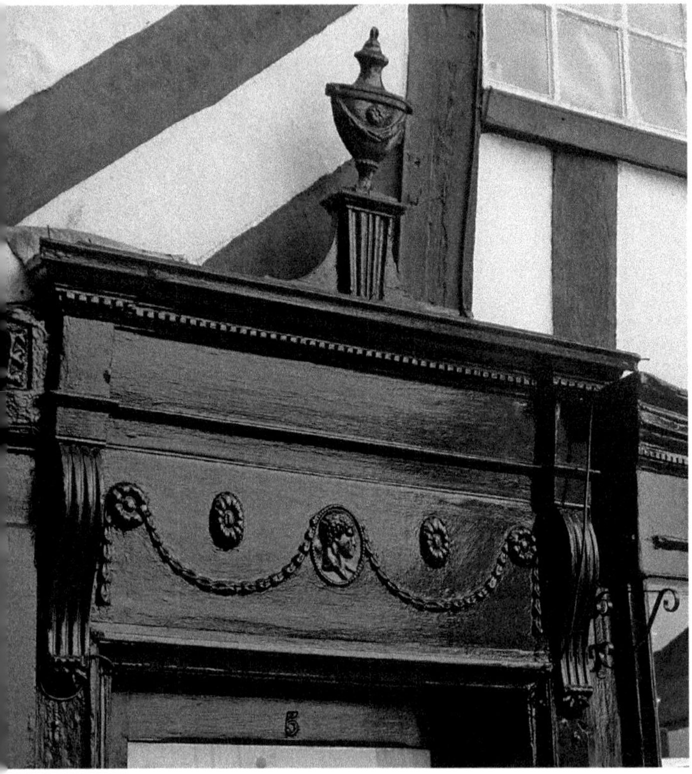

Early nineteenth-century doorway, King Charles House.

frontage, as shown on an engraving of 1799, faced on to the Cornmarket, and the frontage to New Street was secondary. A carved wooden inscription, formerly on the porch, has been reset on the Cornmarket frontage. It reads 'Love God WB 1577 RD Honor Ye Kinge', which does not refer to the reigning monarch at the time (Elizabeth I) but is a biblical (mis)quotation (1 Peter 2:17). The initials are those of William Blagden and Richard Durant. The timberwork includes a mixture of close studding, herringbone framing and square framing.

Only part of the house now survives. The gables were removed in the mid-nineteenth century. The corner of New Street and Cornmarket was rebuilt in brick around 1800 after fire damage. Note the unfinished brickwork to the higher parts of the walls, suggesting an unrealised intention to rebuild the rest. The frontage of the New Street section (now the King Charles House pub) was rebuilt around 1670, and the gables were reinstated in 1986 after another fire.

King Charles House has the best collection of eighteenth- and nineteenth-century shopfronts in Worcester. These include bowed and multi-paned shop windows and an unusual wide sash window, while one doorway has delicate Regency decoration including a Pompeian urn over.

In New Street a profusion of panelling and carved woodwork is nearly all imported from other buildings, including an elaborate wooden chimneypiece from Sidbury House, demolished in the 1960s.

17. Nos 18–20 Silver Street (the Old Infirmary)

Across a wide expanse of roads and car parks, this remnant of Silver Street feels rather detached from the city centre. Yet medieval Silver Street was an important link between the city centre and Lowesmoor, and the road to Droitwich. This unprepossessing building is the last survivor of the historic street, and for a quarter of a century housed one of eighteenth-century Worcester's most important amenities: the city's first hospital.

The industrial suburb of Silver Street and Lowesmoor grew from around 1200 in the valley of the Frog Brook, which drained the low-lying marshy area east of the walled city. Tile making was a speciality here, including decorated floor tiles and later roof tiles. Later, bricks, clay pipes and bells were made here.

The suburb was levelled by the Royalists in the Civil War, as part of the effort to defend the city. The buildings here are a rare survivor of the first generation of rebuilding after the war, a pair of brick houses with rear workshops, built in 1677.

Following the Dissolution of the Monasteries, hospital provision (outside London) had been very poor. It was only in the eighteenth century, with growing urban populations, that public health became an important issue. Groups of volunteers started setting up hospitals, at first in existing (and often quite unsuitable) buildings, in an early move towards a comprehensive health service.

Below left: The restored frontage of Worcester's first infirmary, Nos 18–20 Silver Street.

Below right: The building in 1951. (Worcester City Council)

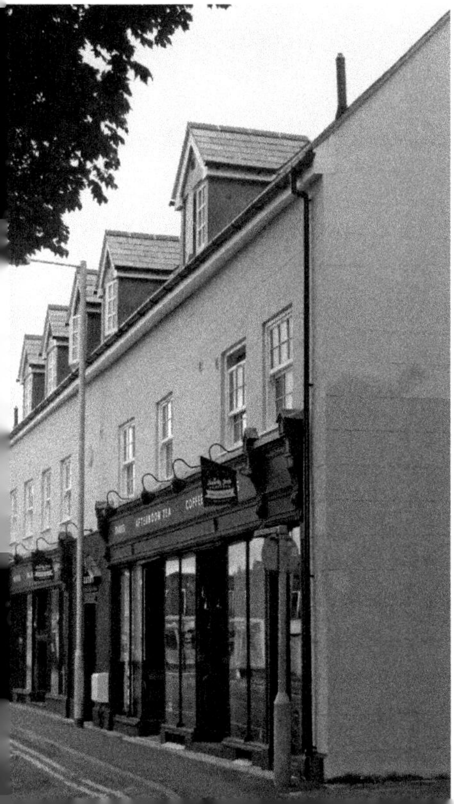

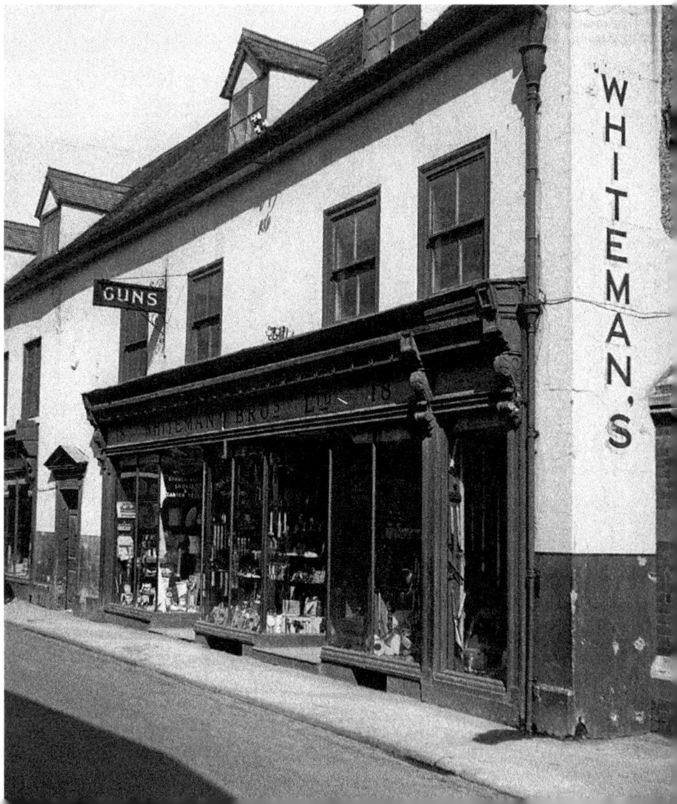

Worcester's hospital opened in 1746, and subscribers (who paid 1 guinea annually) were able to recommend one in-patient and one outpatient each year: 'none are admitted unless curable, and real objects of charity' (Valentine Green). Wealthier people would at this time have been treated at home. Worcester's Old Infirmary may be the last survivor in England of this first generation of hospital buildings. It was replaced in 1772 by the purpose-built infirmary in Castle Street.

Although the front part of the building has been heavily altered, in the rear wing, the large windows, makeshift wooden cubicles and carved initials on the timbers all offer a unique and fascinating glimpse into the world of eighteenth-century health provision.

18. Hill, Evans & Co. Vinegar Works: the New Filling Hall

From small beginnings, the Hill, Evans & Co. factory near Lowesmoor grew to be one of the world's largest vinegar breweries. Vinegar brewing began in this industrial area around 1800. The Hill, Evans partnership took over in 1830, and expanded the works through the nineteenth century. Many buildings were lost following closure of the vinegar works in 1964, and others demolished to make way for the St Martins Quarter development. However, enough survives to maintain a Victorian character on the site, and allow its history to be traced.

The New Filling Hall from Pheasant Street.

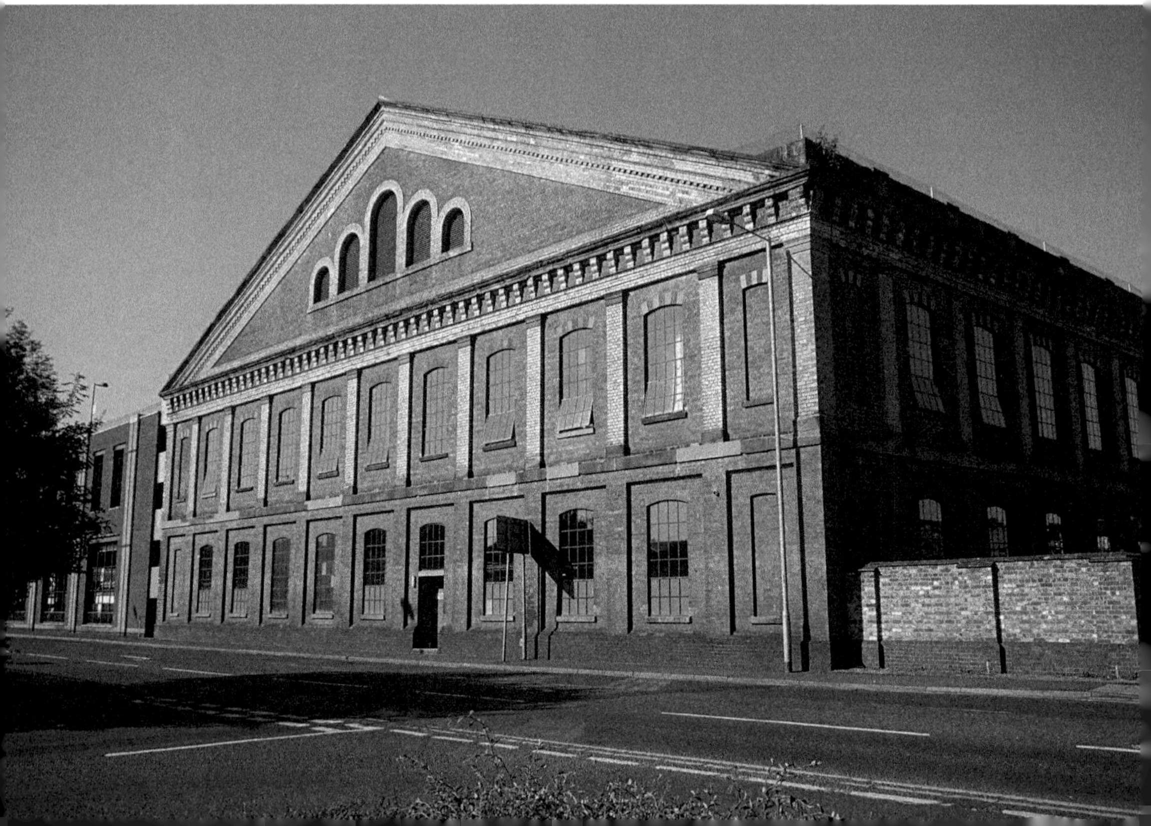

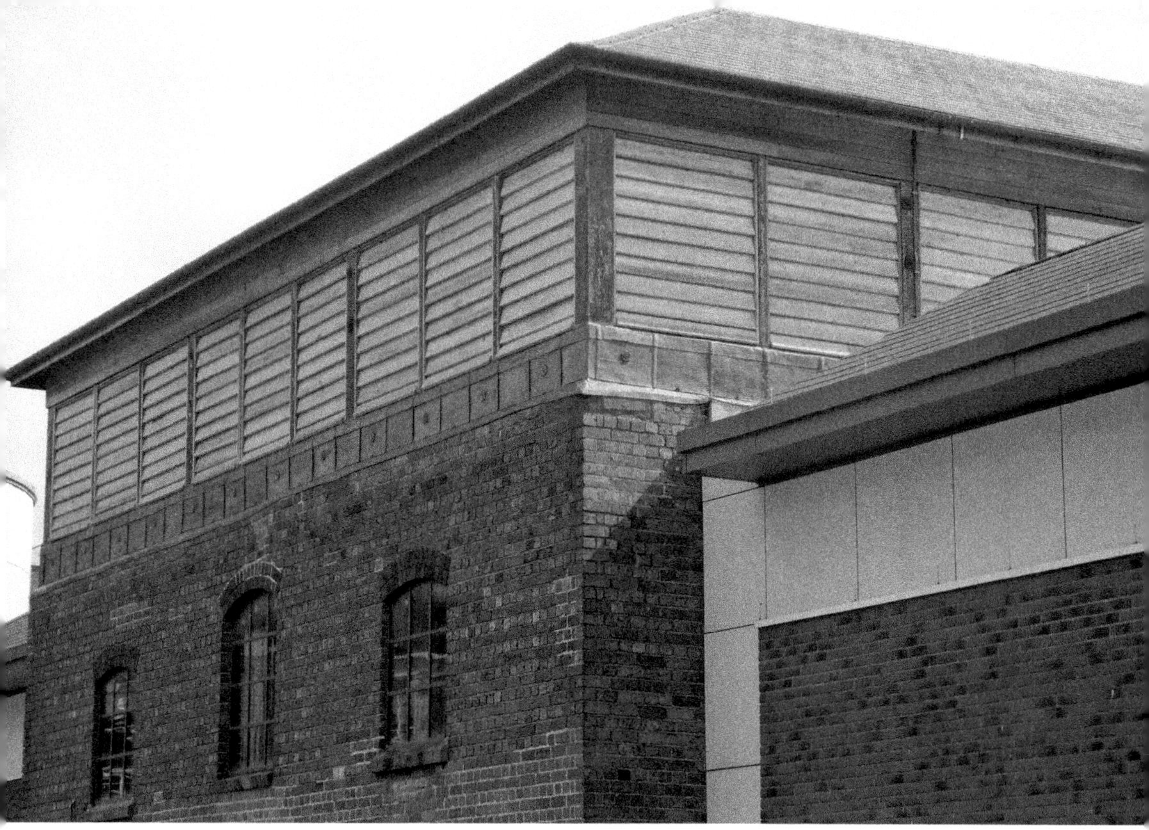

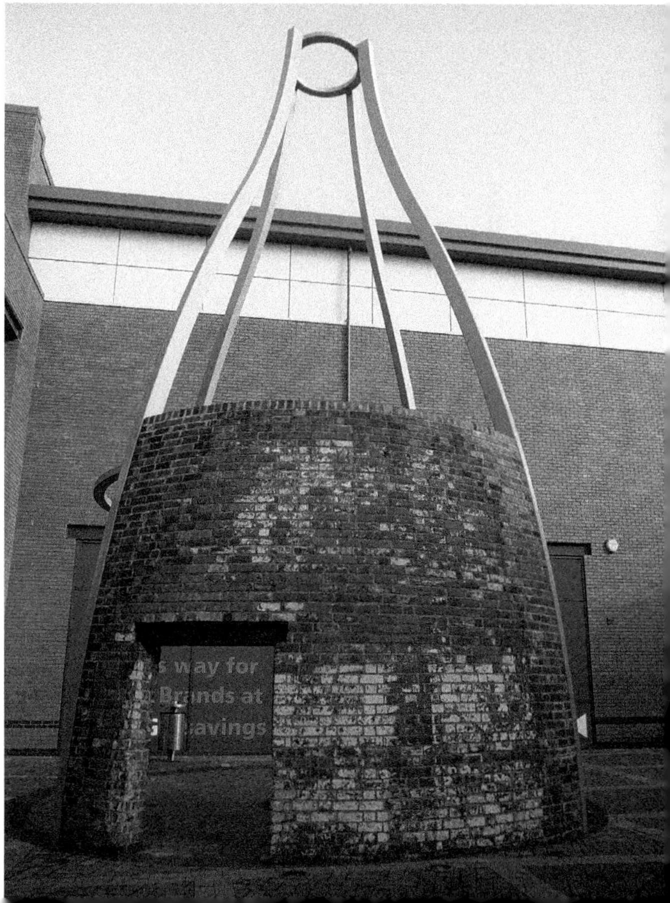

Above: The roof and louvres of the Fermenting House.

Right: The reconstructed kiln hovel, Grainger's porcelain works, St Martin's Quarter.

Although vinegar manufacture is similar to beer brewing, the process is much slower. A series of buildings of the early 1860s replicated a Victorian tower brewery, but here the stages were in separate buildings, side by side. Of these, the granary (due to become a church) and the fermenting house, with its louvred openings to allow the wild yeasts in, survive. The Tudor-style counting house (office) is now the entrance to Asda. Towering over it is the New Filling Hall (late 1860s), marking the end of the vinegar process. Huge vinegar vats, said to have been the largest barrels in the world, stood in the massive open space. Smaller barrels were filled here and left the site on the 'Vinegar Express', the railway that linked the works to the main line. The polychrome brick façades and massive pediments make this Worcester's most imposing industrial building, and its new use as an army base has retained the open central space to the roof. Below the Asda supermarket are large ranges of vaulted cellars, which were used for maturing British wines, also made here. One cellar retains traces of use as an air-raid shelter in the Second World War.

In the nineteenth century, industry extended from the city walls up to Shrub Hill. Next to the vinegar works was Grainger's porcelain factory (*c.* 1804–1901), now represented by a former showroom and the reconstructed remnants of Worcester's last bottle kiln hovel. Foundations of other kilns survive below the modern shops.

19. Queen Elizabeth House, The Trinity

Trinity Street and The Trinity recall the guild that occupied this quarter of medieval Worcester and gave its name to one of the gatehouses. Suppressed in 1546, the Trinity Guild had a guild hall, chapel, almshouses and large gardens within the walls, and was an important charitable organisation, helping the poor and supporting the grammar school, as well as contributing to the upkeep of the bridge and the city walls. The fifteenth-century Old Bridge House is the sole survivor of the medieval complex, though much rebuilt, and some other buildings remained until a century ago. The almshouses survived the suppression, and by the late nineteenth century extended from here to the corner of St Swithins Street, in a district of narrow lanes and alleyways.

Queen Elizabeth House is a truncated remnant of the almshouses. Built in around 1554, just two bays survive. There is a balcony surmounted by two gables, while on the ground floor an alleyway, now filled with a glazed doorway, cut through the building (this was formerly The Trinity). In 1891 it was decided to preserve the building by moving it on rails to make way for a road scheme.

The building gets its name from a story that Elizabeth I addressed the people of Worcester from its balcony when she visited the city in 1575. If she addressed the public at all, it would surely have been at the Guildhall, and it seems unlikely that she would have come here.

Queen Elizabeth House has had many uses over the years and is now offices.

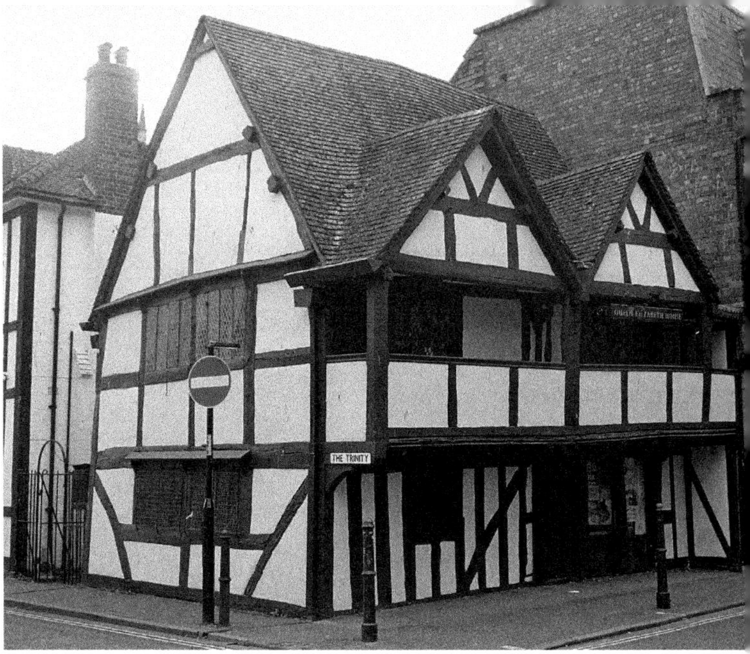

Queen Elizabeth House.

20. St Swithun's Church, Church Street

The east end of St Swithun's Church has the most elaborate frontage, providing a grand bookend to Mealcheapen Street. From the High Street, the west tower is partly hidden behind later buildings. In common with All Saints, St Nicholas and St Martin, St Swithun's was largely rebuilt in the eighteenth century. Unlike the others, the rebuilding in 1734–36 was partly in a Gothic style, the tower with its ogee windows and stone panelling contrasting markedly with the classical style of the body of the church. The architects were Thomas and Edward Woodward of Chipping Campden.

The origins of St Swithun's are unknown, but there was a church here by 1126, sited over the corner of the long-disused defences of the Anglo-Saxon burh. The medieval church must have been roughly the same size and shape as the Georgian one. The sandstone north wall is at least partly medieval. The fifteenth-century tower largely survives, encased in Cotswold limestone, though there is no sign now of the octagonal upper stage shown on early maps. A clock crowns the east gable, though remarkably its mechanism is at the west end, in the tower.

Inside, the church is aisleless with a wide nave. The plaster ceiling is decorated with bosses and corbels, and the floor is covered with ledger slabs over burial vaults.

There is a full set of box pews, their plainness contrasting with the elaborate pulpit and adjacent mayor's chair complete with mace stand. The pulpit is topped with a carving of a pelican 'in her piety' (the mother drawing blood from her breast to feed her young). On the west gallery is a restored eighteenth-century organ, which is still used for recitals.

St Swithun's was declared redundant in 1977. It is currently being restored by the Churches Conservation Trust, with the aid of lottery funding, as a music and arts venue.

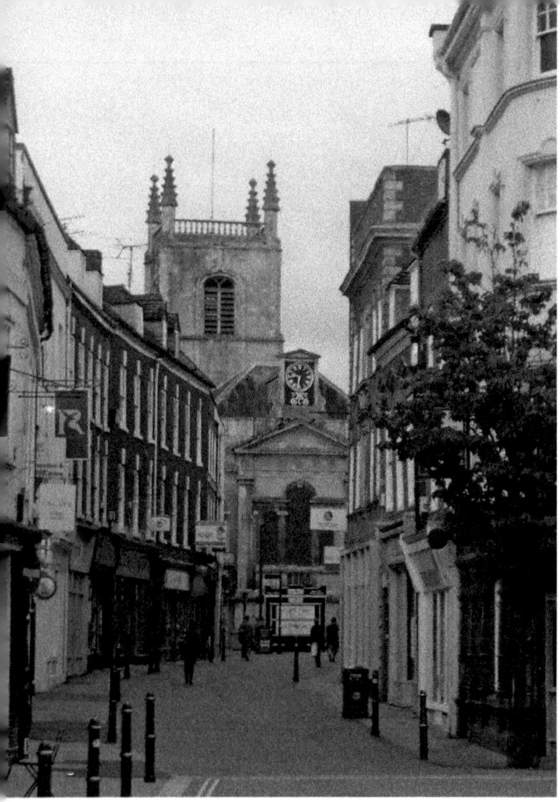

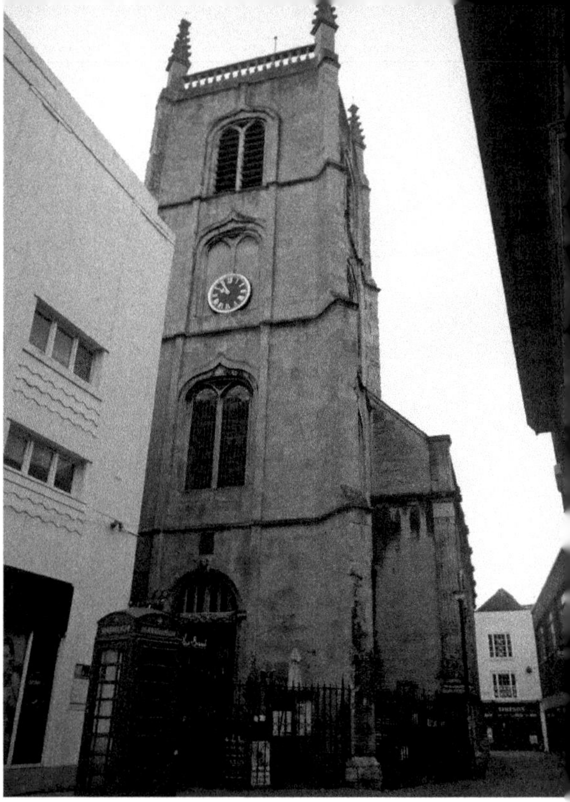

Above left: Mealcheapen Street and the east front of St Swithun's Church.

Above right: St Swithun's Gothic tower.

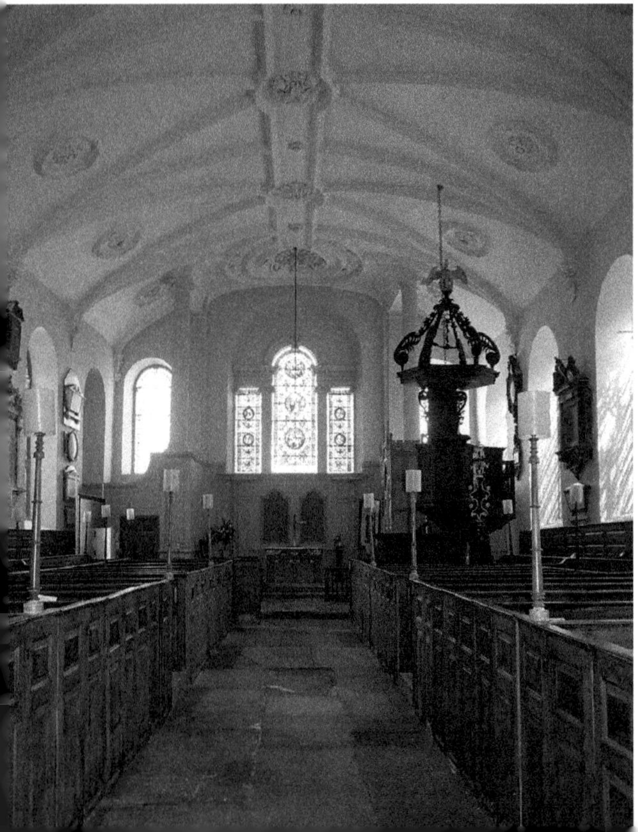

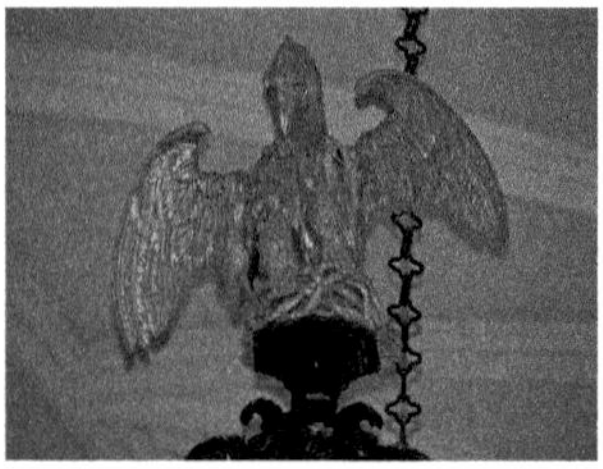

Above: The pelican over the pulpit.

Left: St Swithun's interior.

Below: One of many cherubs in St Swithun's.

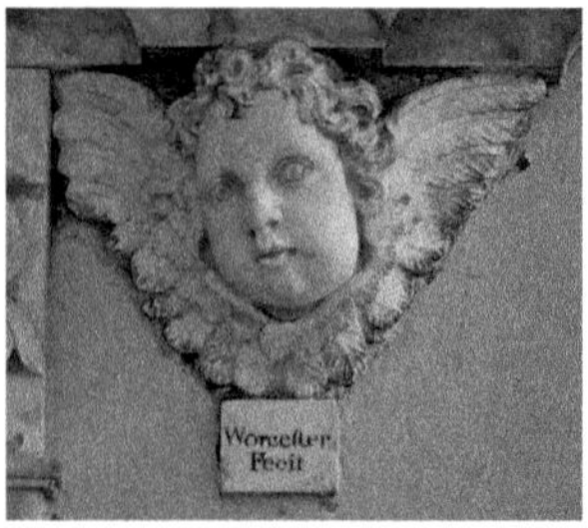

The adjacent brick building, now a restaurant, was the schoolroom of the Royal Grammar School, which was rebuilt in 1735. The school moved to its current site in the 1860s.

21. No. 61 Broad Street (Cupola House)

Worcester has many grand Georgian houses, but this one in Broad Street must be the oddest. There are six storeys from the cellar to the domed Gothic belvedere on the roof, but the building is only a single bay wide. For a long time it has been a puzzle – some thought the domed room was a private synagogue – but new research has shown that it was lived in, and probably built by, Joseph Blackburn, an eighteenth-century painter. Blackburn was a well-known society portraitist, first in Bermuda (from 1752) and then in New England. Many of his portraits are

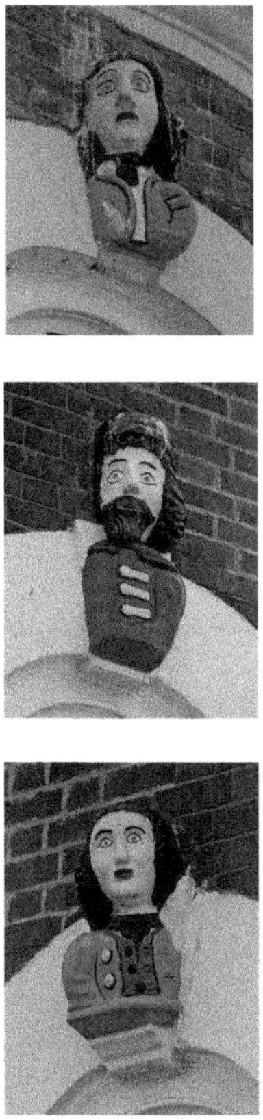

Above: The three keystones.

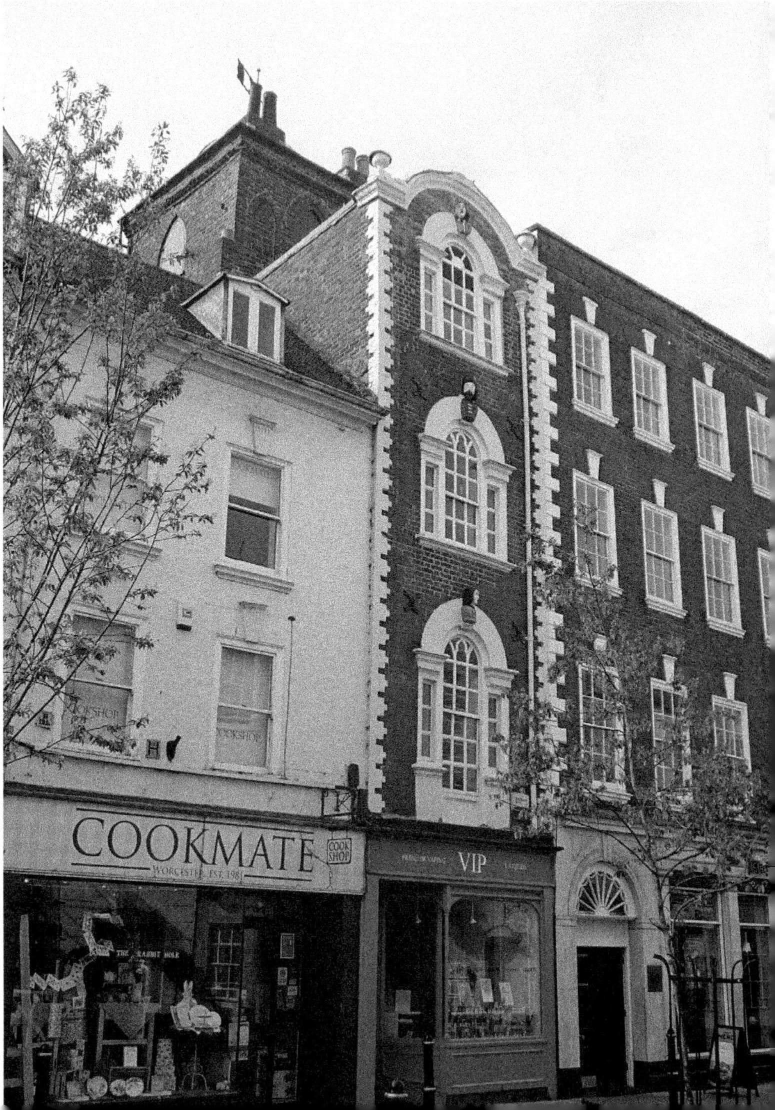

Right: No. 61 Broad Street.

in public collections in the United States. He also taught the more famous painter John Singleton Copley. Blackburn came from Worcester, and he returned to the city with his family in around 1764. The Blackburn connection could provide a plausible explanation for both the external and internal features of this very unusual building.

The red brick of the façade is typical of Worcester in the Georgian period, as are the stucco quoins. Above a modern shopfront, three Venetian windows are each surmounted with a painted head. These may well recall Blackburn's travels across the Atlantic. Inside there is a Chinoiserie staircase, extending the full height of the building, and much decorative woodwork and plasterwork.

Broad Street was laid out in around 1200 along the outside of the disused Anglo-Saxon burh defences, and the burgage plots along the south side of the street, including this one, extended over the infilled ditch, which was found in excavations in 1989.

22. Lloyds Bank, The Cross

The former head office of the Worcester City and County Bank is the very model of a trustworthy local bank headquarters, modelled on a Florentine palazzo (recalling the medieval bankers of that city), brick built and solidly faced in

Lloyds Bank and St Nicholas' Church, The Cross.

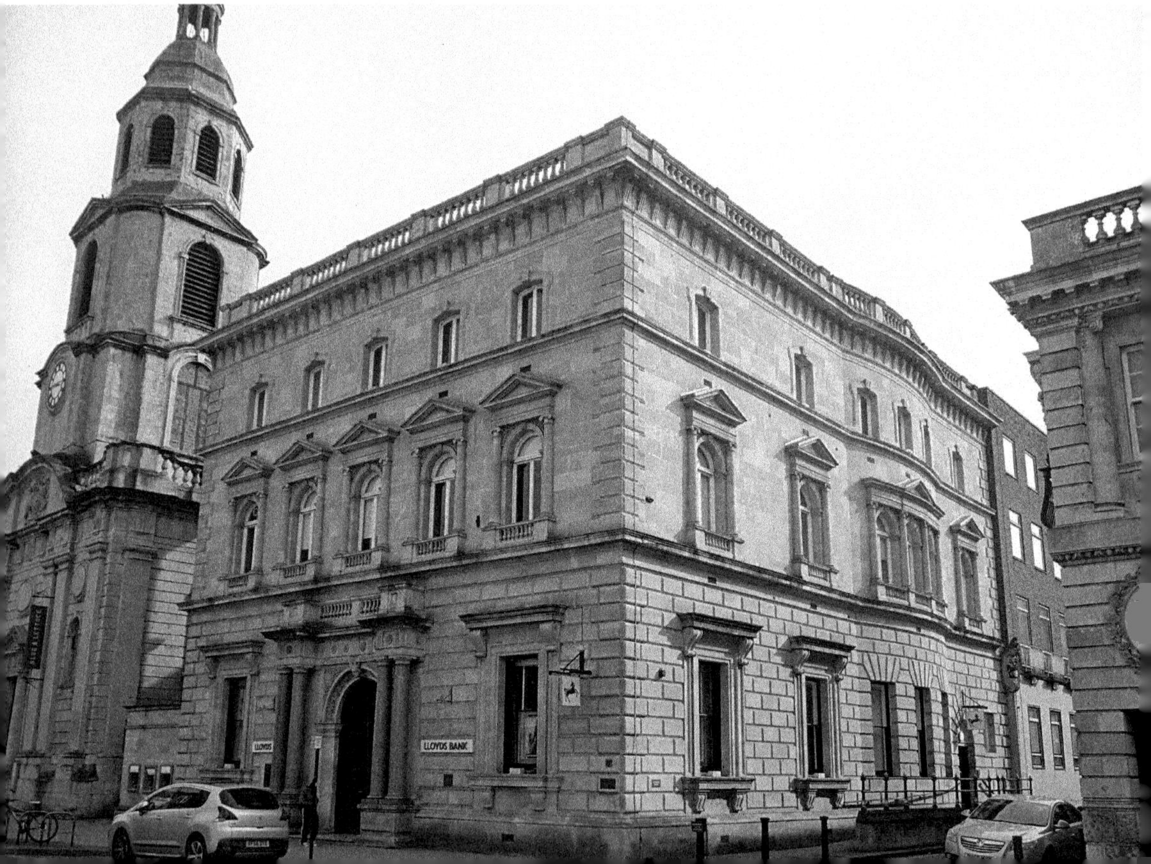

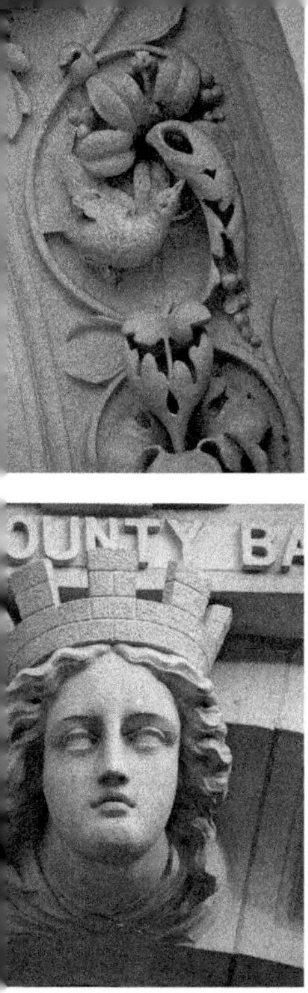

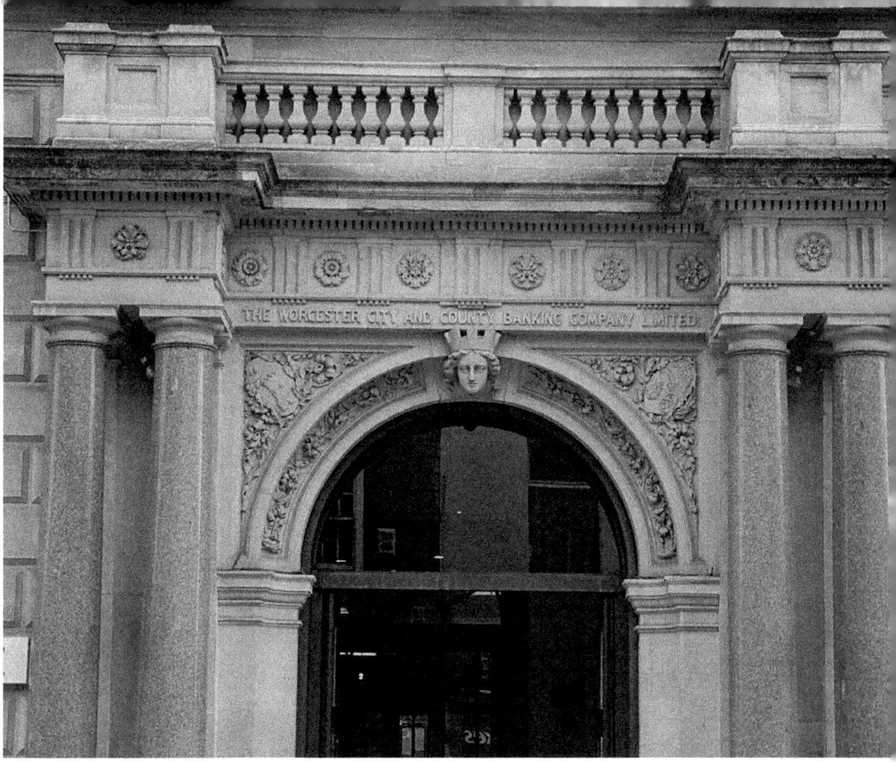

Above left: Details of the Forsyth carvings, Lloyds Bank.

Above right: The main doorway of Lloyds Bank.

Cotswold stone. It was designed by Edmund Elmslie of Malvern and built in 1861–62. The bank was founded in 1840 and merged with Lloyds in 1889.

The Cross was one of Worcester's many marketplaces and its width (less obvious now since the streets around have been widened) provided the perfect stage for this substantial building, which stands next to St Nicholas' Church, also faced in Cotswold stone. Elmslie's building has three storeys, rusticated and heavily quoined, and with the roof hidden by a parapet. Windows have pilasters and heavy stone surrounds with large scrolled corbels.

The entrance is flanked by polished pink granite pillars, and is a showpiece of the work of William Forsyth. The keystone is a crowned head, while to either side are carved shields and roundels with plant scrolls and birds. Other decorative carvings can be seen on the window surrounds, and there is further Forsyth work in the vestibule.

23. Corn Exchange, Angel Street

Medieval and early modern cities had many markets, both general and specialised, and wholesale as well as retail. Worcester had several markets specialising in the agricultural produce of the county: livestock, grain and other crops. Corn exchanges provided a wholesale market for grain crops, and many towns saw new buildings erected in the mid-nineteenth century.

The Corn Exchange in Angel Street was designed by Henry Rowe and built in 1848. A rival exchange was opened in 1849 in the Cornmarket, but after a short life became a concert hall.

The massive Tuscan columns on the building's façade make a powerful statement of the economic importance of farm produce in Worcestershire's county town, with gilded sheaves of corn decorating the parapet either side of the 'Corn Exchange' sign. The interior, visible through the large doorway and display windows, is a single large open space, now with an inserted gallery. The exchange fell out of use by the end of the nineteenth century and was later used as an auction room, while boxing matches were also held here. Following restoration in the 1980s, the building became a shop, and later a restaurant, but is currently empty.

This was a busy commercial area in the nineteenth and early twentieth centuries. To the left of the Corn Exchange is a contemporary four-storey hop warehouse, which still retains its hoist beam, loading doors and platforms to all the upper floors, and a hop press. To the rear is a medieval house, later used as a warehouse, (now part of a pub), the red sandstone wall of which can be glimpsed down the alleyway on the left-hand side. Meanwhile, the building opposite, on the site of a former sheep market, was opened in 1920 as a market hall for fruit and vegetables.

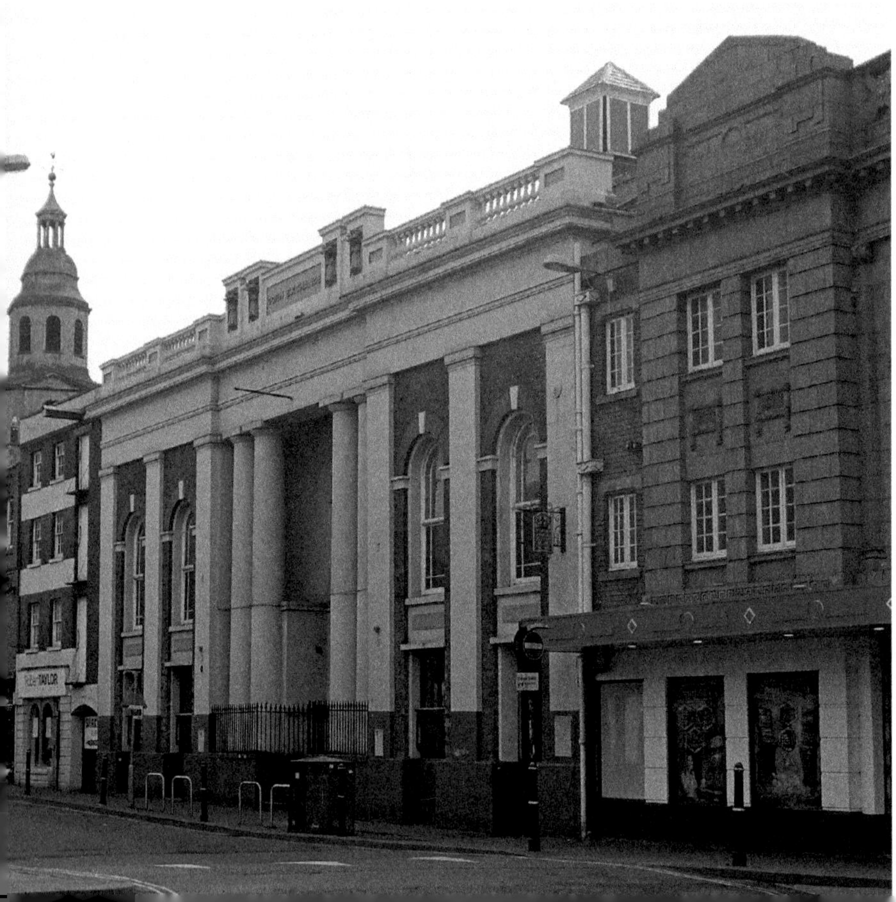

The Corn Exchange, Angel Street.

24. The Hopmarket, The Foregate

Built over the medieval city wall and ditch, the Edwardian baroque Hopmarket building dominates one of Worcester's busiest crossroads. As with Berkeley's Hospital (opposite), the abandonment of the medieval city wall and ditch, within a few decades of the Civil War, created new opportunities for development. On this site, what came first was Worcester's first workhouse.

Worcester had a hop market as early as 1670 (in the Cornmarket) and the income from the market supported the workhouse. When a new workhouse was opened at Shrub Hill in 1794, moving the hop market into the vacant building must have seemed obvious. The hop trade in Worcester grew steadily through the eighteenth and nineteenth centuries, influenced by factors such as the growth of large brewers and the export of beer to India, while Worcester supplanted other markets to become the only place in the Midlands where hops were traded. Hop merchants' offices and warehouses surrounded the market. At the end of the century it was decided that a new purpose-built market was needed. The present building, complete with warehousing, a hotel and a bank, was designed by Alfred

Below left: The Hopmarket.

Inset: The Hopmarket Hotel sign.

Below right: Cupola at the corner of The Foregate and Sansome Street.

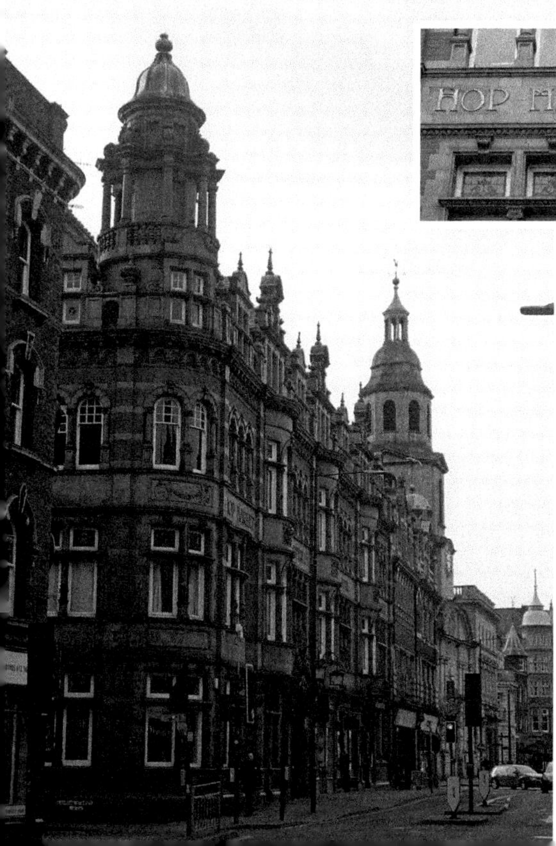

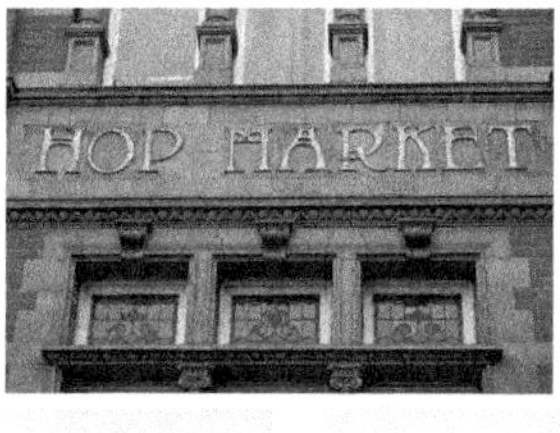

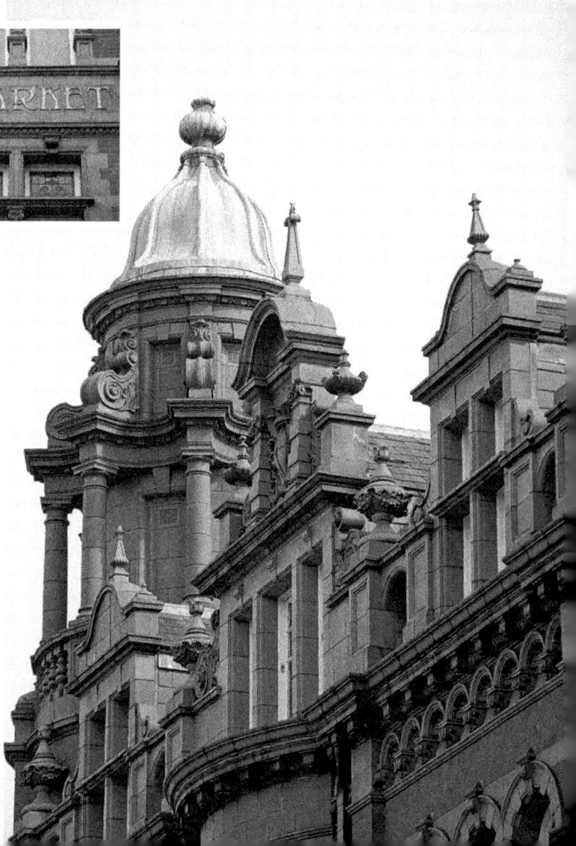

B. Rowe and opened in 1900. The rebuilding also allowed the widening of The Foregate to make way for tramlines, and other buildings followed in the first decade of the twentieth century.

The market building encloses a courtyard where the hop sales took place, which is now surrounded by small shops and cafes. The hop trade had changed by the mid-twentieth century and the market became redundant. Worcester City Council redeveloped the Hopmarket in 1979.

The Hopmarket combines elements of classical antiquity – Doric and Ionic capitals – with styles borrowed from the Tudor period and the baroque chateaux of the Loire, and much use of orange Doulton terracotta. Cherubs and swags of hops decorate the façade where the Hop Market Commercial Hotel and Bank are proudly announced in art nouveau lettering. The roofline is finished with multiple shaped pediments, urns and a colonnaded cupola to the corner in contrasting red-brown terracotta.

25. Berkeley's Hospital, The Foregate

Thousands must pass Berkeley's Hospital every day without a second glance. Yet the almshouses are among Worcester's finest buildings, and would not be out of place in Amsterdam or Bruges. They may have been inspired by a visit Robert Berkeley of Spetchley had made to the Low Countries.

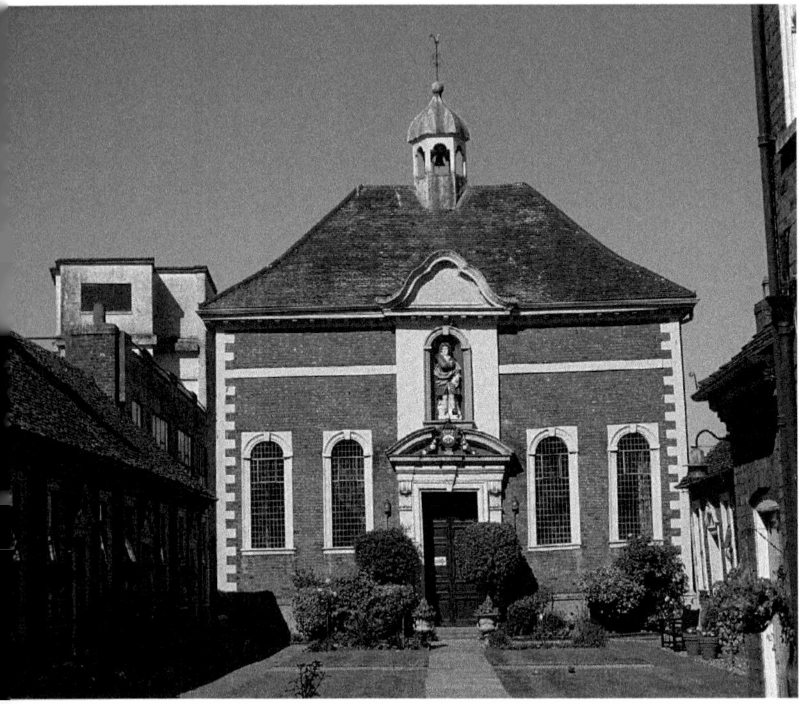

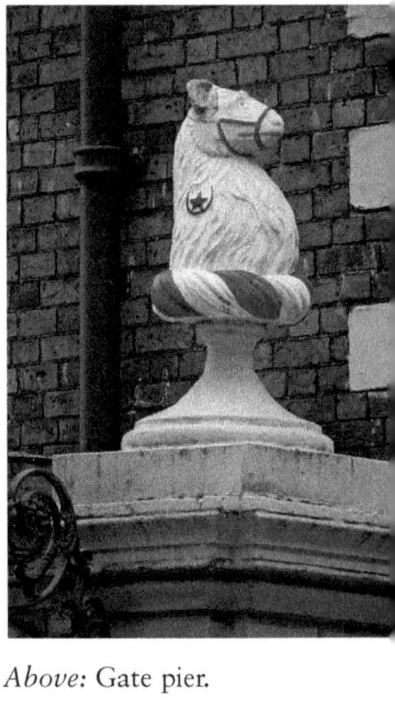

Above: Gate pier.

Left: The chapel and almshouses of Berkeley's Hospital.

Berkeley endowed the almshouses in 1692. The adjacent Foregate was demolished in 1702 and the chapel is dated 1703. The buildings were completed by around 1710. The Berkeley badge is prominent on the gate piers, which are topped with haltered heraldic bears.

Here again, a new use was made of the land formerly occupied by the city defences. The almshouses were built largely over the infilled ditch, partly over the demolished wall and gatehouse. The ditch fills have settled over three centuries, and the two rows of houses now lean gently inwards towards each other.

Towards the street are two-storey lodges, once occupied by a warden and a chaplain. The single-storey almshouses range five on each side of the central courtyard. Throughout, decorative doorcases display the Berkeley arms.

The chapel, with its round-arched windows, hipped roof and lantern, dominates the little courtyard from the far end, and is now a community room. We are once again reminded of Berkeley's generosity by his statue in a niche on the façade, 'in his robes, well-executed' (Green).

26. The Hop Pickers, Sansome Street

The offices of Sydney Myer, hop merchant, were in a prime location, directly opposite the Hopmarket. In building his new office here in 1875 (designed by Haddon Bros), Myer chose the most dramatic and substantial

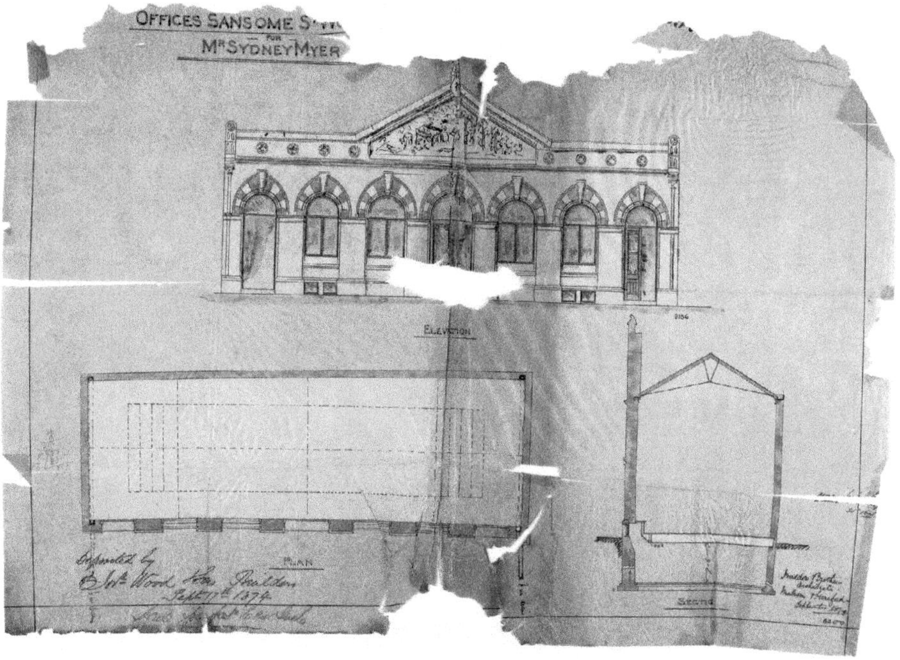

Building application plan for Sydney Myer, by Haddon Bros, 1875. (Worcester City Archives)

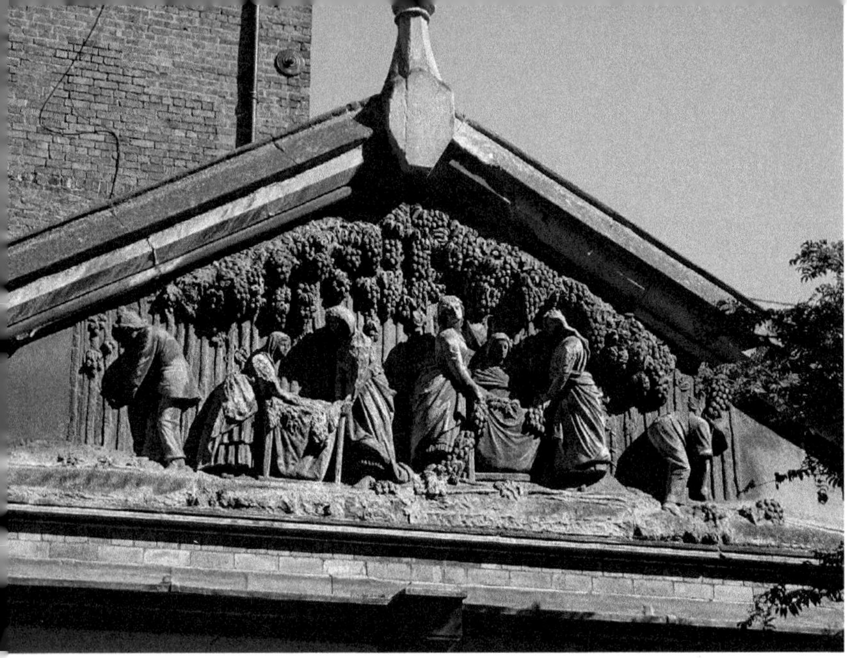

William Forsyth's Hop Pickers sculpture.

advertisement medium. The large pediment of the otherwise unremarkable single-storey building (topped with a large foliate finial) is filled with a limestone sculpture depicting a scene of hop picking, and was by Worcester's leading Victorian sculptor William Forsyth (1833–1915). William and his brother James were born in Kelso in the Scottish borders, and trained in London before moving to Worcestershire to work on the fountains at Witley Court. James Forsyth moved back to London where he developed a national practice, while William remained in Worcester, where an elaborate carved shopfront on The Tything marks his workshop. During the later nineteenth century he worked on church monuments and furnishings as well as architectural sculpture. Many examples are still to be seen in Worcester and Malvern.

The Hop Pickers sculpture is one of William Forsyth's major surviving works and a vivid depiction of an idealised Victorian rural scene. At least one member of Forsyth's workshop, the sawyer, is depicted (on the far left), while the right-hand figure is said to be a self-portrait of William. The Forsyths' Scottish origins are referenced in one of the female figures, based on a sculpture of Highland Mary (lover of Robert Burns).

Apart from the sculpture, there is now little other evidence of the building's Victorian past, and sadly weather and vehicle emissions have taken their toll on the surface of the stone, but the scene still makes a powerful impression.

27. The Old Rackets Court, Sansome Walk

The Arboretum district has a very distinctive history, much of which is reflected in the Old Rackets Court. Sansome Walk, on its western edge, was a fashionable promenade, and is still marked by a stone obelisk in the gardens of

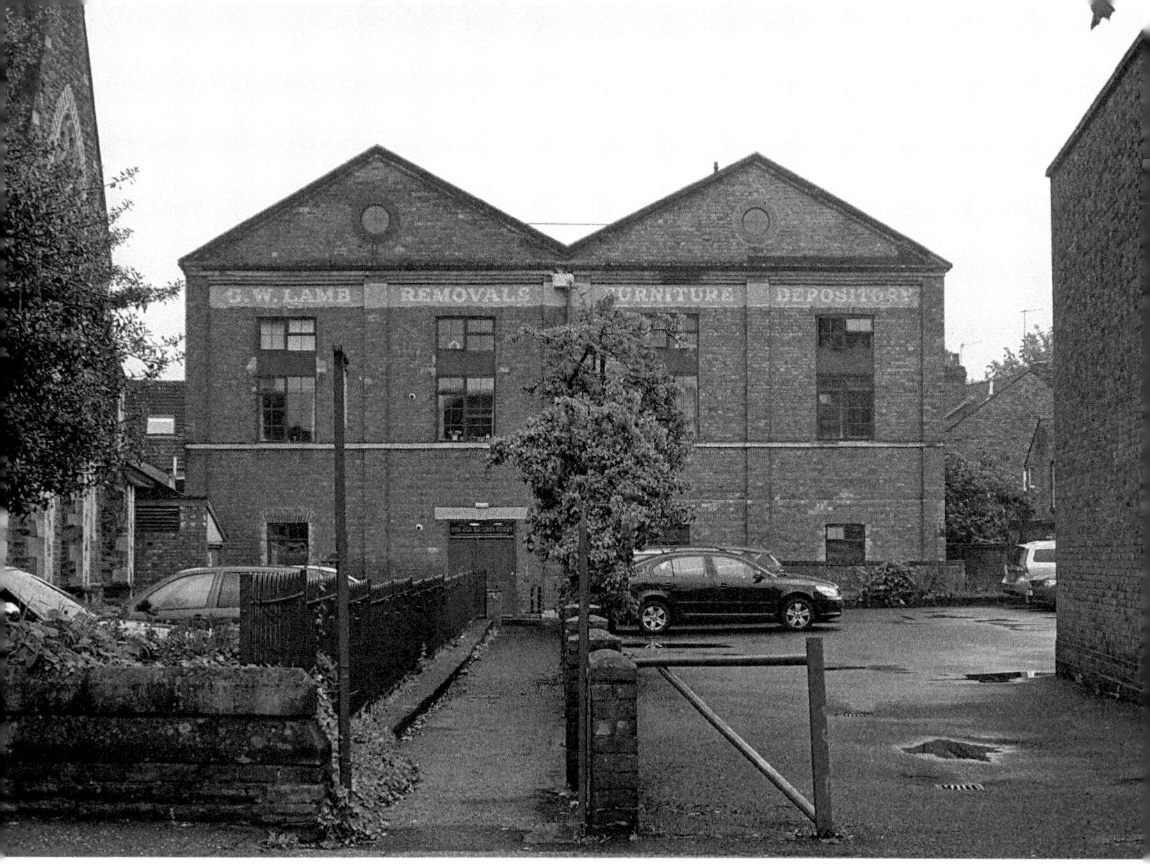

Above: The Old Rackets Court's Sansome Walk frontage.

Right: The heavily buttressed back wall of the first rackets court.

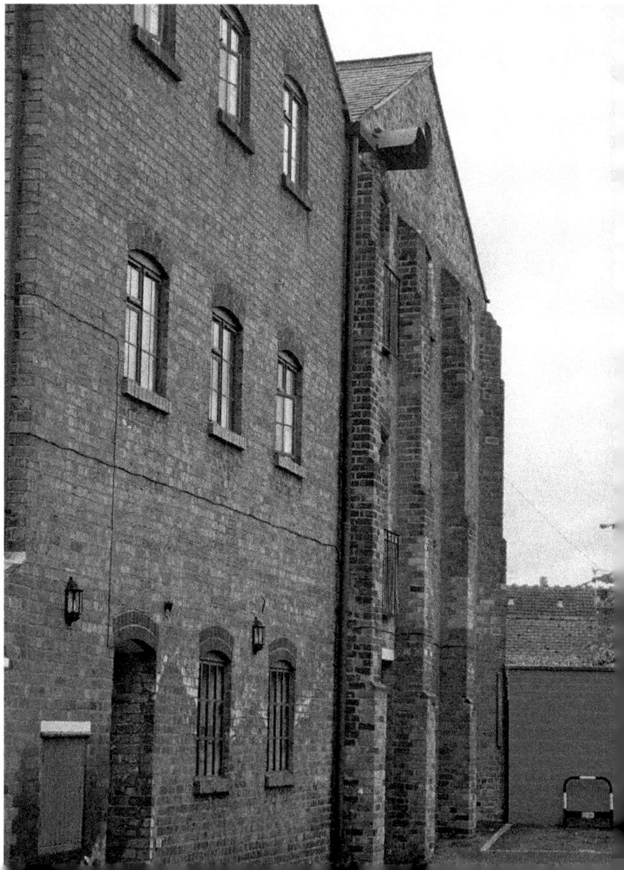

St Oswald's almshouses. In 1859 the Worcester Public Pleasure Grounds Company opened a public garden that extended from Sansome Walk towards the canal. The middle classes subscribed to gain admission; the City Council, who contributed to the project, insisted on free public access, but the owners allowed this concession only on Mondays so it may not have been well used. The venture was not a commercial success and it closed in 1865. The land was sold for development and is now filled with housing. The gatehouse survives, and several of the streets follow the garden walks. Terraced housing for railway and other workers is interspersed with several hop warehouses that tower over the area.

Leisure pursuits continued to flourish in the area after the closure of the gardens, with a roller-skating rink, bowling green and swimming baths, as well as this building, a former rackets court, which has over time reflected the leisure, commercial and residential aspects of the Arboretum.

Rackets was a predecessor of squash, which was first played in London prisons in the eighteenth century. It eventually lost ground to the younger sport, largely due to the expense of building and maintaining the much larger courts, and courts are now very scarce. It could be played indoors or outdoors. In the late 1840s or 1850s an open outdoor rackets court was built here, with a heavily buttressed full-height front wall (30 feet high), and stepped side walls giving a court length of at least 40 feet. This was incorporated into a covered court in 1861, the same size (60 by 30 feet) as the court at Prince's Club in London. There are traces of a spectator's gallery.

The rackets court was out of use by the early 1870s, and was readily converted into a warehouse, with inserted floors and windows, for the hop merchants Caldicott's. The floors are supported by cast-iron columns made by Hardy and Padmore of Worcester. A second warehouse was added alongside in 1878. The specification for the works, drawn up by the architects Yeates and Jones, stipulates timber from Sweden, Russia, and Memel in East Prussia (now Lithuania) and Welsh slate and Broseley ridge tiles for the roof.

The building continued in use as a hop and seed warehouse until 1969. After a period as a furniture repository, it has now, like the other three hop warehouses in the Arboretum, been converted into housing.

28. Museum and Art Gallery (Victoria Institute), Foregate Street

On the east side of Foregate Street stand two imposing nineteenth-century public buildings. The Victoria Institute houses the Museum and Art Gallery and City Council offices. Worcester's first museum had opened in 1833 in Angel Place, and moved to Foregate Street in 1836. A new purpose-built museum was designed by J. W. Simpson and E. J. Milner Allen, the architects of Kelvingrove Museum in Glasgow, and built in 1894–96. The city's library was also here until the opening of the Hive.

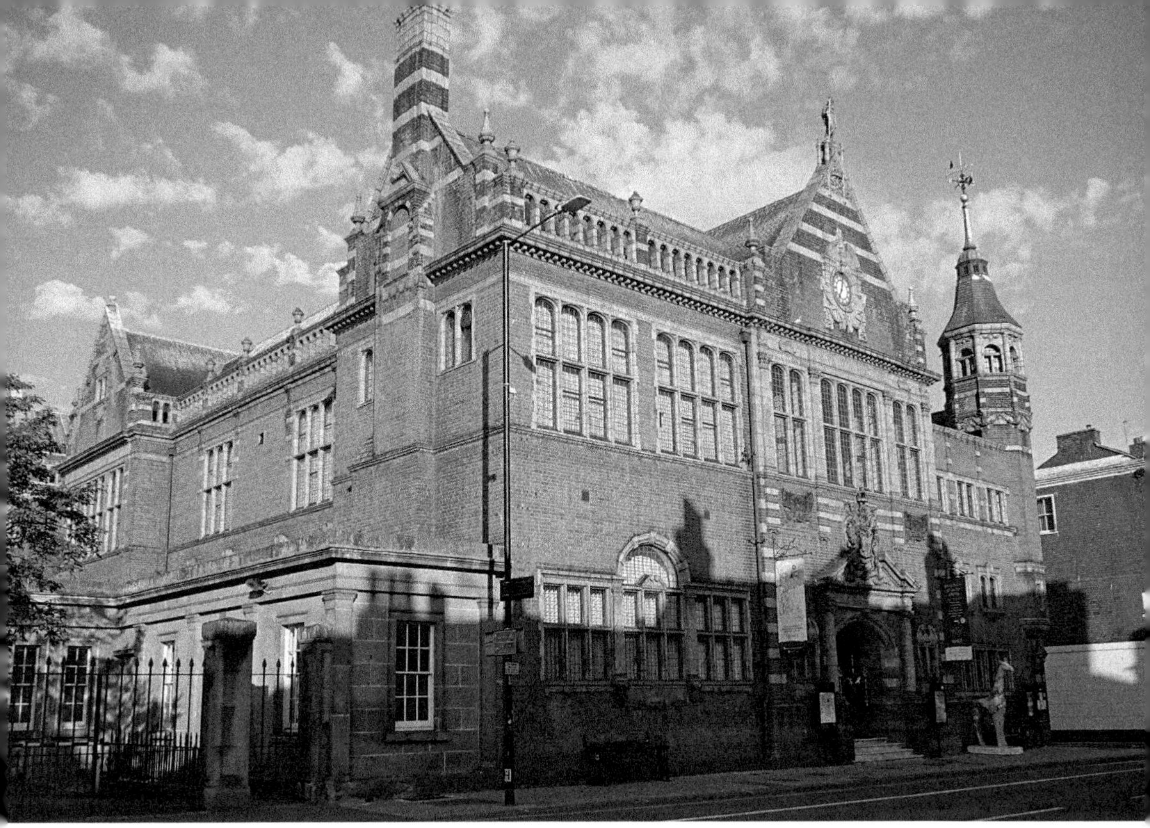

Above: Victoria Institute's Foregate Street façade.

Below left: The pediment is crowned with a statue of the goddess Victory.

Inset: Moulded brick panel.

Below right: The School of Art and Science, Sansome Walk.

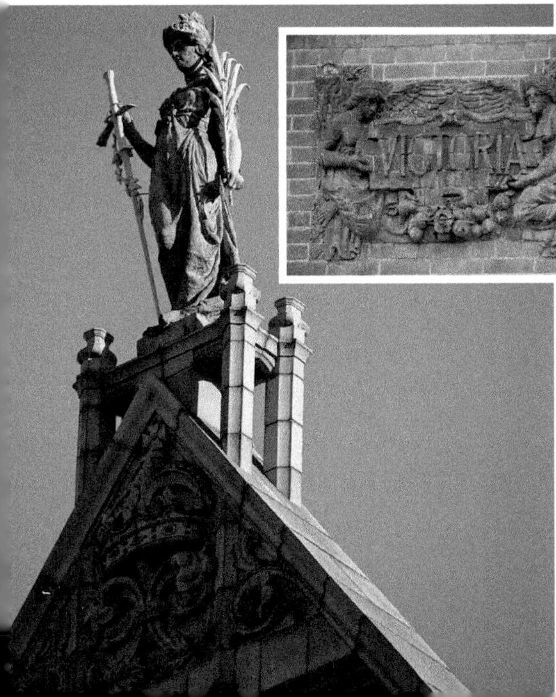

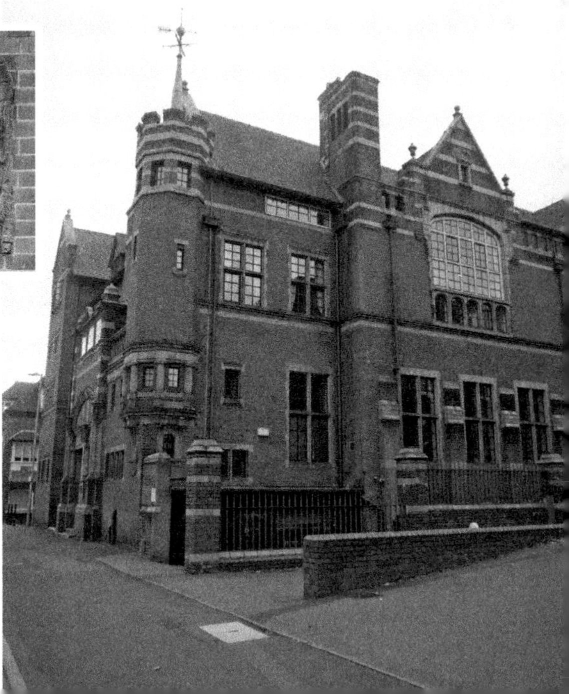

This was towards the end of the Victorian age, and although the building drew on historical styles, it also looked forward to the new century. It is in brick, with stone and Burmantofts terracotta dressings. The style was described as 'Queen Anne ... with Italian modifications', but Tudor, Jacobean and French influences can also be seen. The asymmetrical façade, with its corner turret, is highly decorated with relief panels in brick, including Victoria's royal arms, and the pediment is crowned by a statue of the goddess Victory. The building was carefully extended to the rear by A. G. Parker (1935).

At the rear end of the plot, on Sansome Walk, is the School of Art and Science, also by Simpson and Milner Allen. This again has an interesting asymmetrical façade, with a corner turret and spirelet, but on a smaller scale, and with more Arts and Crafts influence. Terracotta is used for cherubs and bulgy colonettes and for the motto 'The lyfe soe short, the art so long to lerne'. The building was enlarged to become the Girls Secondary School (A. G. Parker, 1909–10), and has now been converted into apartments. On Taylor's Lane is a stone inscription from the seventeenth-century Inglethorpe's Almshouses, which stood on the site.

29. The Shirehall, Foregate Street

On the north side of the Victoria Institute, the Shirehall of 1834–38 is by Charles Day. As with the city's Guildhall, the seat of county administration had multiple functions, with a council chamber, offices and courts. It still serves as the county court.

Shirehall façade, with statue of Queen Victoria in the forecourt.

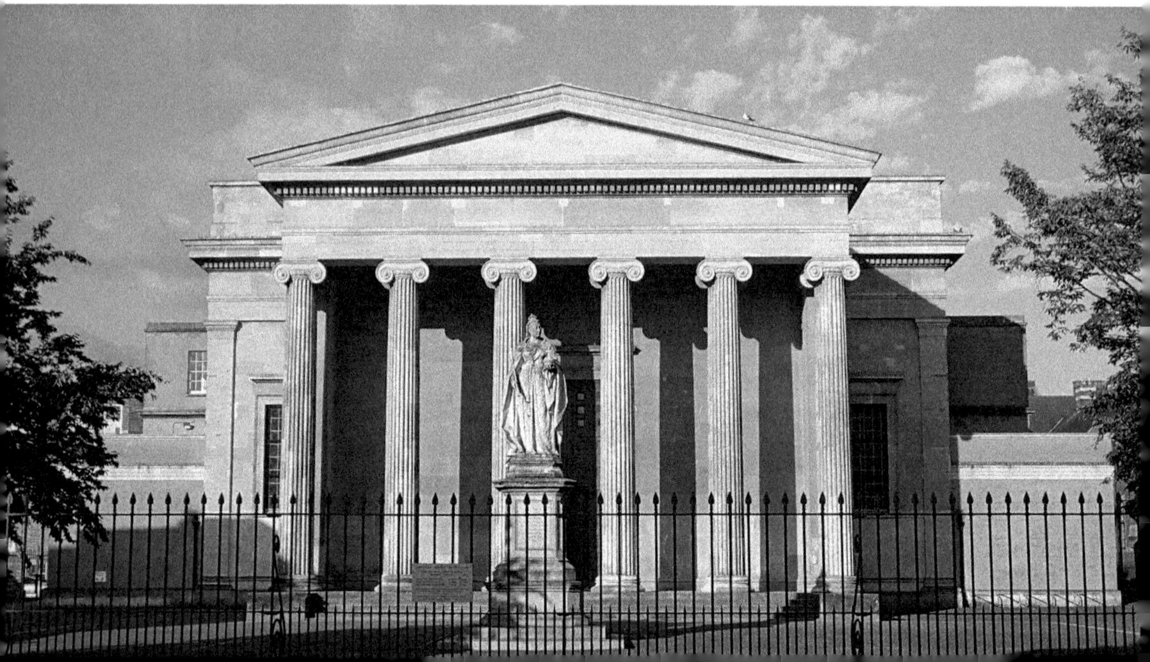

Its most memorable feature is the grand Grecian portico, with six giant Ionic columns. Inside, the former County Hall has an impressive display of heraldic stained glass of around 1909.

Behind the Shirehall is the contemporary judges' lodgings (by Day, 1834–35, and Henry Rowe, 1898). This is in brick, with Doric detailing, and linked to the Shirehall by discreet additions by Associated Architects in 1995. Completing the ensemble at the front are gate lodges, also by Day and Rowe.

In the forecourt, the statue of Queen Victoria commemorates her golden jubilee in 1887. The sculptor was the Worcester-born and trained Thomas Brock, who later sculpted the national memorial to Queen Victoria in front of Buckingham Palace.

30. Austin House, Castle Street

Dutch and Scandinavian influences can be seen in the design of this former garage, in particular its distinctive tower, a well-loved landmark. The garage was built on the site of the former City and County Prison (opened in 1813, closed in 1922), whose castellated gatehouse gave the street its name. The building has recently been refurbished for the art and illustration departments of the University of Worcester.

The architect was John Carrick Stuart Soutar, architect to H. A. Saunders, Austin dealers of North London, and also to the Hampstead Garden Village, and the garage was built in 1938–39. Small stone obelisks are set on the corners of

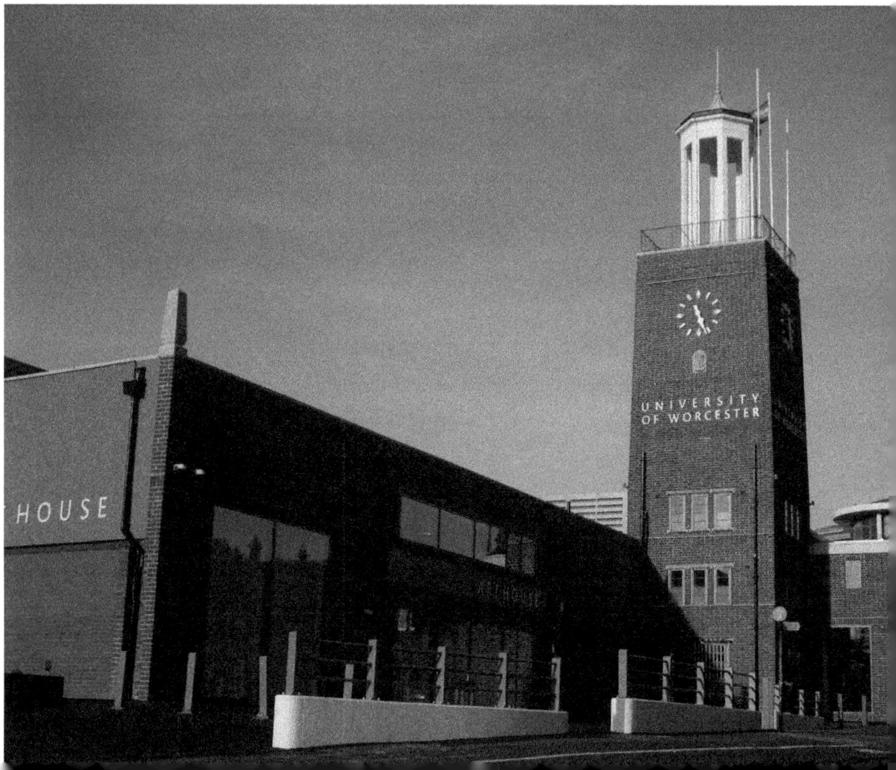

Austin House, now the University of Worcester Art House.

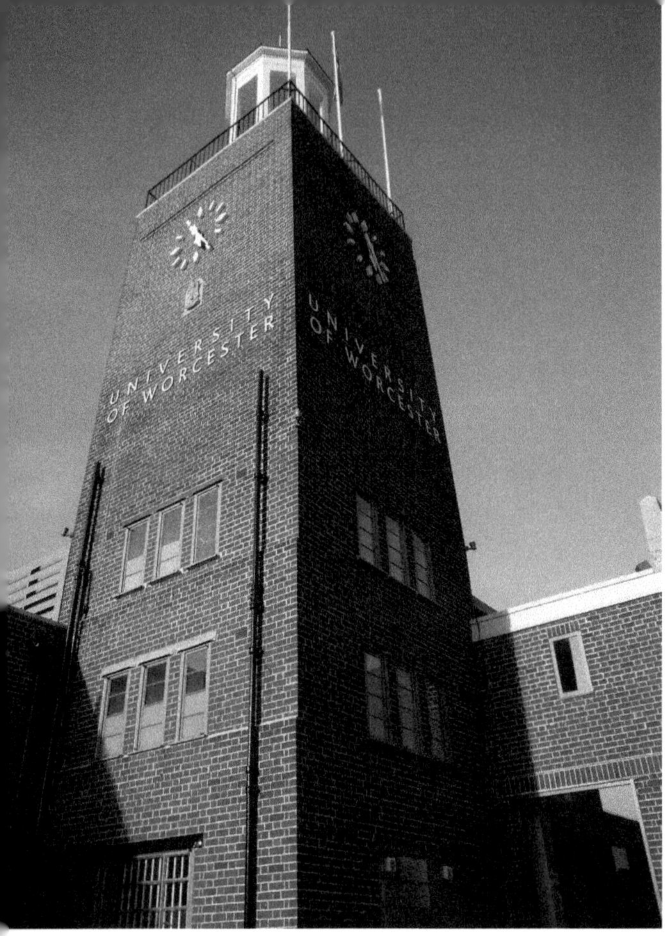

The Austin House clock tower.

the staggered façades of the two main blocks (showroom on the right, workshop set back on the left), which are linked by the tapering brick clock tower, which is topped with a copper-roofed open cupola.

31. Worcester Infirmary (University of Worcester)

Worcester's second hospital was built on the edge of the city, and opened in 1772 to replace the much smaller infirmary on Silver Street. Anthony Keck won the architectural competition. The plans seem to owe much to Gloucester Infirmary (by Luke Singleton) and also to Henry Keene, one of the unsuccessful competitors (Keck also seems to have used a design by Keene when he rebuilt St Martin's Church a couple of years later). Worcester Infirmary remained in use for well over 200 years, only being replaced by the Worcestershire Royal Hospital at the beginning of the twenty-first century. The Georgian infirmary now forms the centrepiece of the University of Worcester's City Campus.

The infirmary as first built had a simple H plan. The red-brick building had two storeys over basements, and contemporary illustrations show pediments and a roofline similar to today. The main entrance was to the east, where the

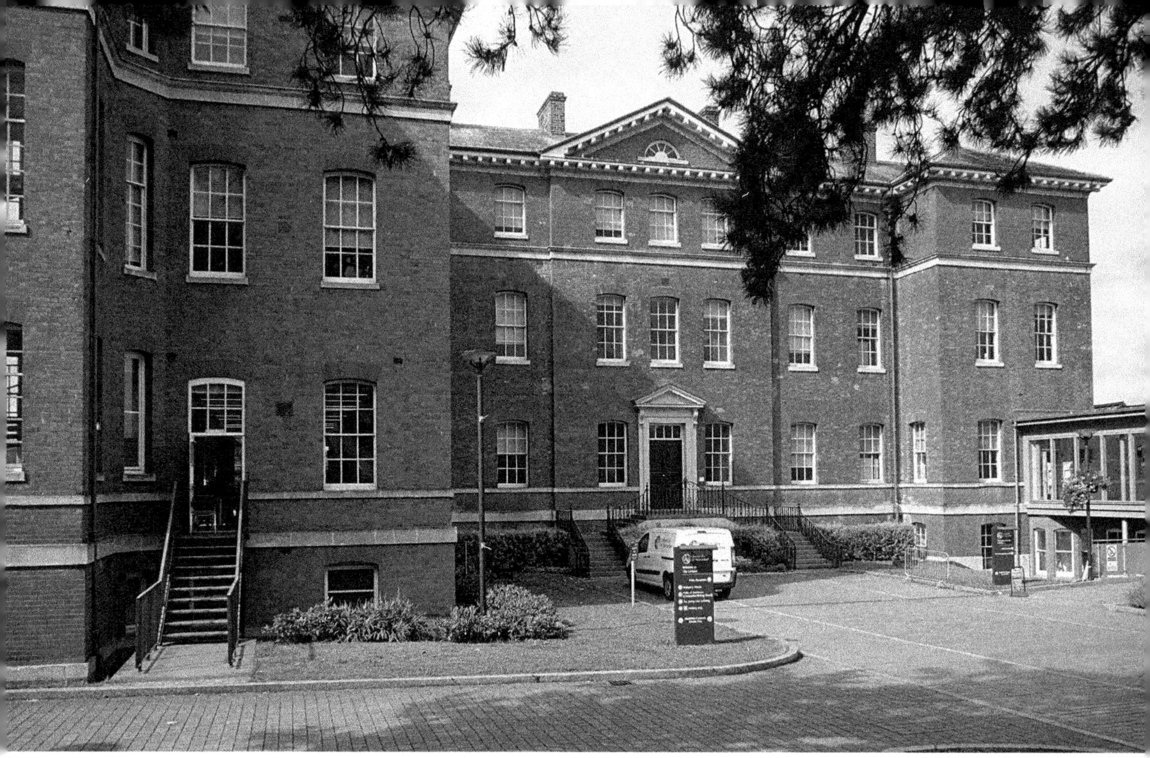

Above: The main front of the infirmary.

Below: The Jenny Lind Chapel and west front.

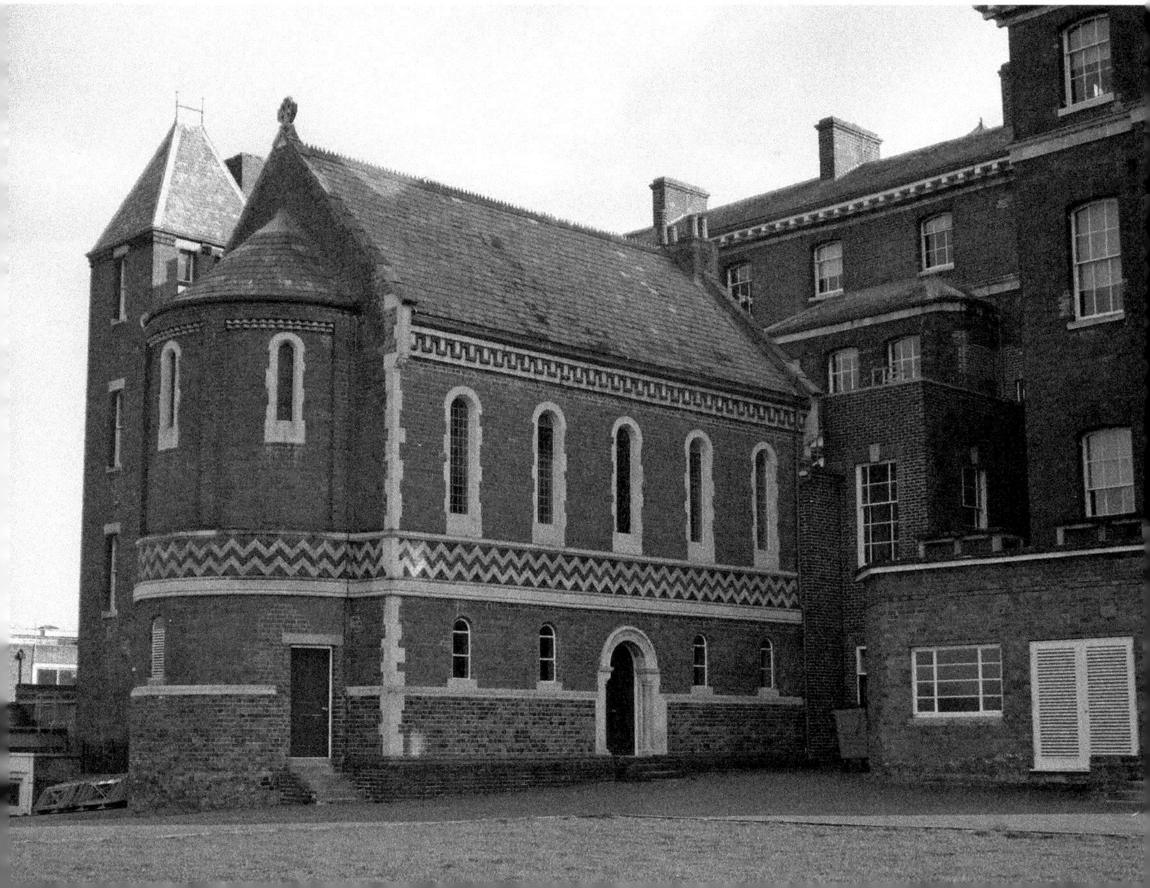

original hallway with its stone-flagged floor survives. On the south façade is late eighteenth- century graffiti, including a peacock.

Extensions to the main building were added at various stages in the nineteenth century. The boardroom was enlarged and the chapel added by Henry Day in 1849–50. The little west-facing chapel was funded by a concert given by Jenny Lind. Now stripped of twentieth-century accretions, the neo-Norman building again holds pride of place on the west side of the infirmary, where its four-colour polychrome brickwork, stone trimmings and subtle use of relief contrast with the earlier buildings. Day added an extra storey to the infirmary in 1864–66. The original stone cornice now forms a string course and a new cornice was formed in white brick. Corner service towers were added in the 1870s and 1880s. Facing Castle Street is the former outpatients department (now a gym), and next to it a stone-dressed baroque wing of 1912.

The initial meeting of the British Medical Association was convened in the boardroom in 1832 by Charles Hastings, then a leading surgeon at Worcester. Hastings was known for his promotion of medical training, and kept meticulous records of the incidence of disease.

In 2009, during redevelopment of the site for the university, archaeologists found two pits containing human bones. Many of the bones displayed cut marks from surgical training. Some had been mounted for anatomical display, and others were from amputated limbs. A tunnel below Castle Street linked the adjacent prison to the infirmary, and it is said that the bodies of executed prisoners were sometimes brought here for anatomy demonstrations. Ten plaster heads, thought to be death masks of prisoners, were found in the tunnel in the 1950s, and are now on display in the George Marshall Medical Museum.

From the 1890s onwards new buildings went up to cater for the needs of the growing city. Mulberry House (1897–98, by Lewis Sheppard), is a well-mannered piece of late Victorian neo-Georgian. Built as a nurses' home, it was overshadowed for most of the twentieth century by larger nurses' homes of the 1930s, but these have now been demolished, along with the twentieth-century childrens' wards, operating block and other buildings.

32. The Paul Pry, The Butts

The Paul Pry is an exceptionally well-preserved backstreet pub from the turn of the twentieth century, which is highly decorated both inside and out. Designed by Frederic Hughes for R. Allen & Sons (the Barbourne Brewery, a new enterprise when the Paul Pry was built), the building makes the most of an awkward 'flatiron' site between The Butts and Infirmary Walk, with a bay window at the apex. From the street, the carved stonework frieze and oriel windows (incorporating the brewer's initials and the date 1901) and etched glass give a hint of the elaborate decorations within. The lobby and passageway have tiled walls and marble intarsia floors.

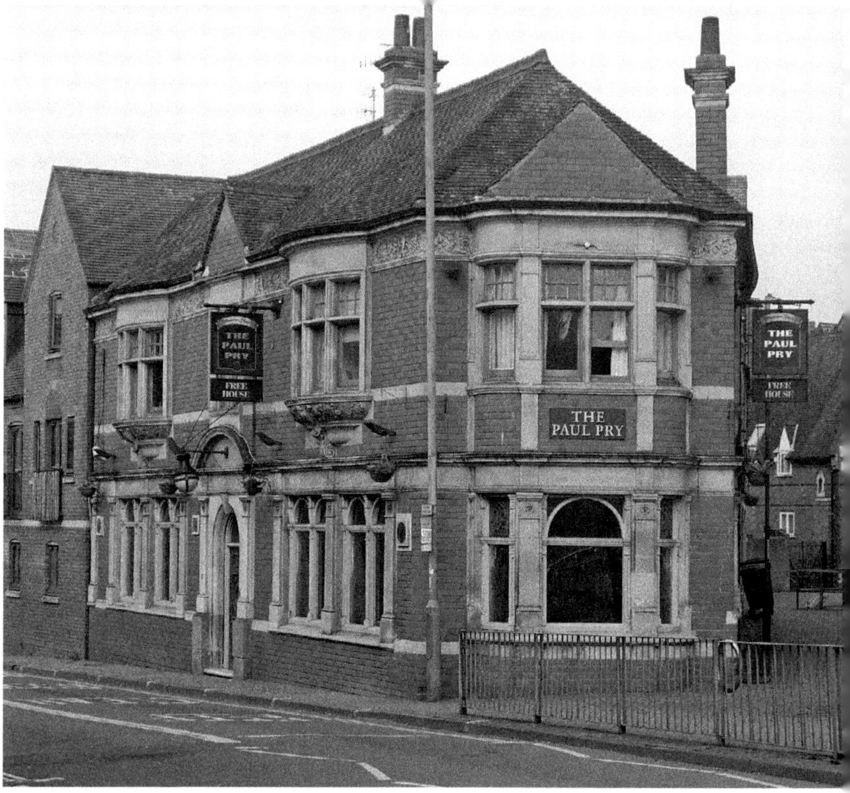

The Paul Pry.

To the left is a (relatively) plain lounge. However, the best decoration is to be found in the bar to the right, at the narrow end of the site. Here, original wall benches, fireplace and flooring survive, and the mahogany counter is overlooked by a magnificent bar back complete with mirrors, a clock and decorative urns.

There has been a pub of this name here since the early nineteenth century. Paul Pry was a busybody, the title character in a popular but now little-known play by John Poole, which was first performed in 1825. Many pubs in England were named after him, and Chamberlain's Worcester factory was one of several that produced figurines of the character.

33. The Hive

When Worcestershire County Council planned a new library for Worcester, the former builder's yard then occupied by the city council's bin lorries in The Butts may not have seemed the obvious site. However, the University of Worcester was starting to develop its campus next door, and the council and university saw the opportunity to create a joint public and university library here. The resulting building, named The Hive after a public competition, opened in 2012, and houses the public and university libraries, the city's public service desks, and the county archives and archaeological service.

With its gold-tiled walls and roof and golden bridge across The Butts, The Hive is surely Worcester's most distinctive twenty-first-century building. Initially its

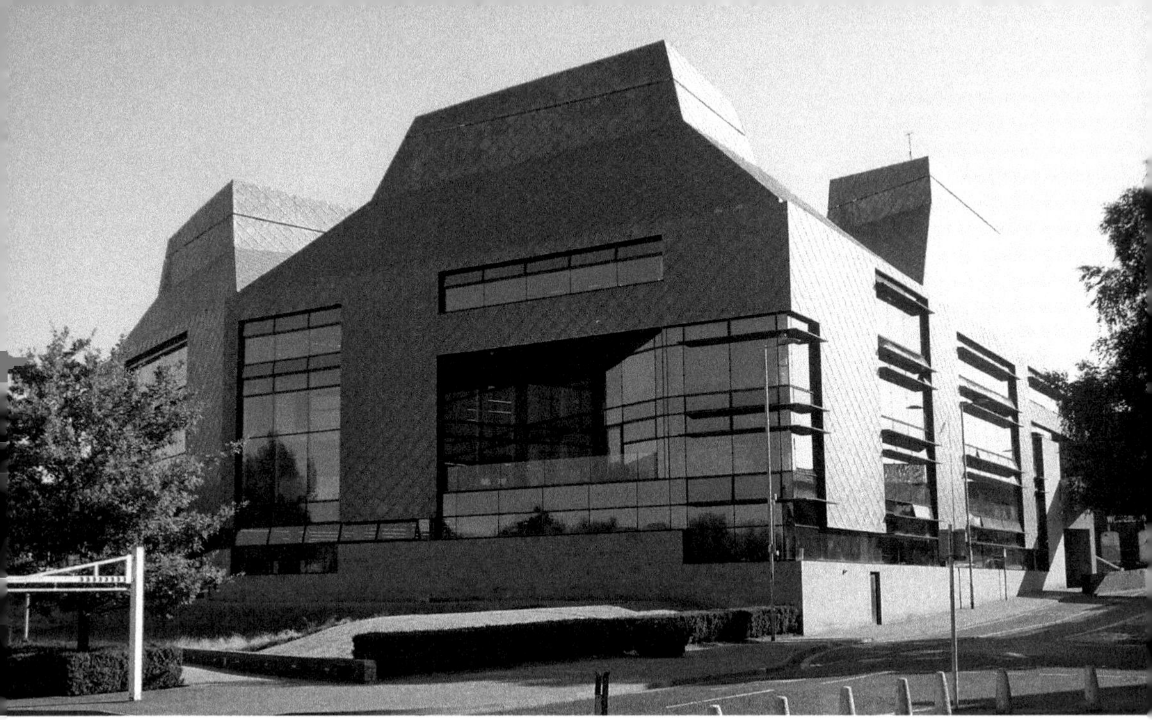

Above: View of The Hive from The Butts.

Below: The Hive from Crowngate.

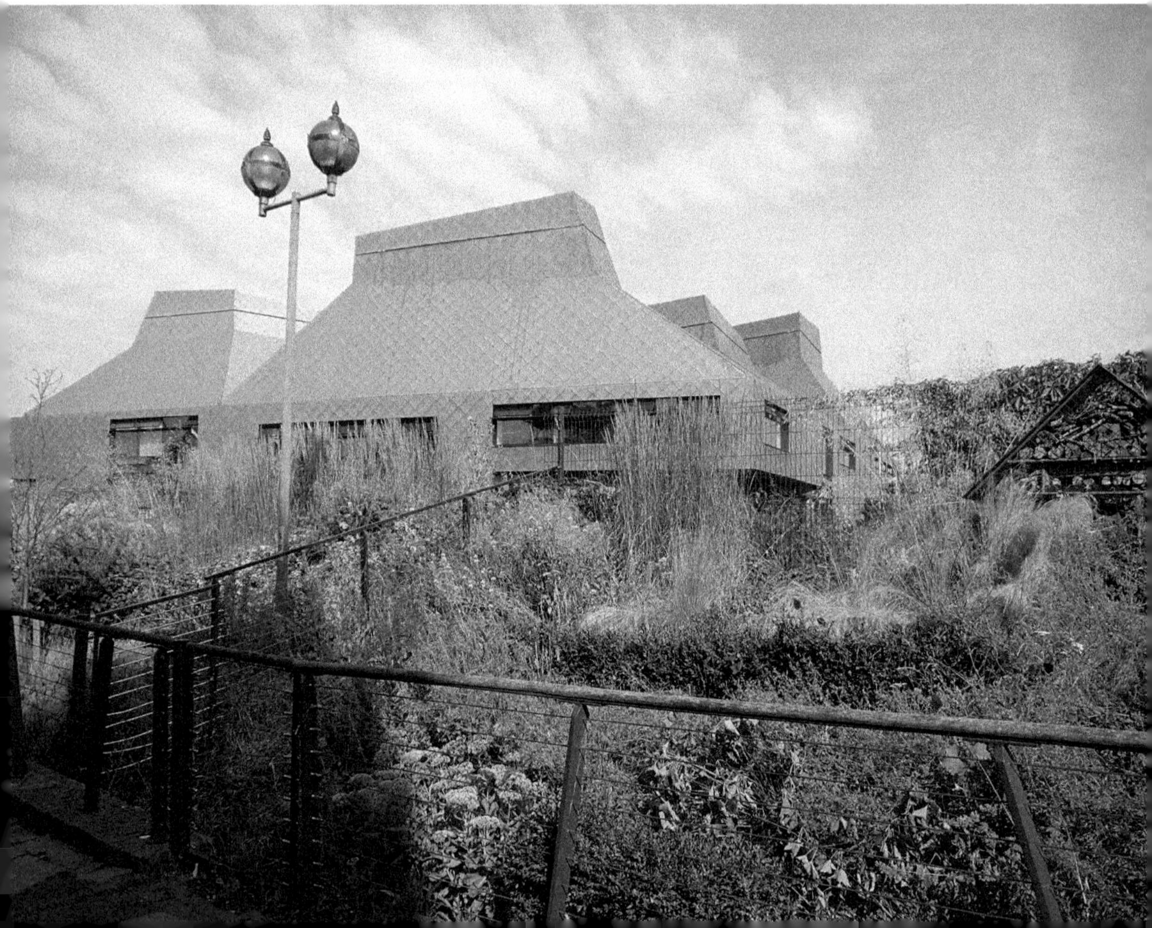

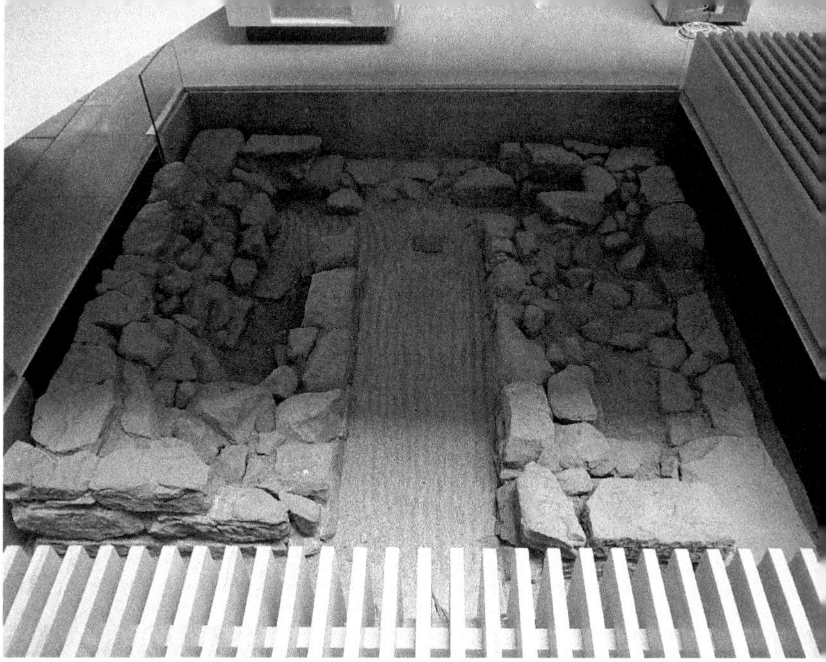

The Roman kiln in The Hive.

appearance seems to have divided the people of Worcester, though most have now taken it to their heart. The product of the turn-of-the-century Private Finance Initiative, the building was designed by Feilden Clegg Bradley Studios and has won many awards. It has many of the latest environmental features including a heating system using water pumped from the Severn and a biomass boiler – there is even a small biomass plantation. The building's landscaped surrounds have been designed to interpret many aspects of the landscape of the county and the history of the site, including the plan of almshouses that stood here and a small panel of Roman iron slag. The form of the building is said to have been inspired by views of the Malvern Hills and the former kilns of Royal Worcester Porcelain. The roof vents are a functional part of the system, drawing air through the interior.

The services housed in The Hive are usually widely scattered. On the lower floors, largely out of sight, are work areas for archivists and archaeologists, and archive stores with 19 kilometres of shelving for documents. Not least, in an era when library facilities and hours are being cut everywhere, the public benefits from the long opening hours of a university library.

Since the building of the medieval city wall just to the south, this part of Worcester had been a marginal area of workshops and builders' yards – the street name (The Butts) refers to archery butts set up just outside the city. However, in the Roman period this area was very much within the town, and an archaeological excavation before the site was developed provided an opportunity for hundreds to take part or visit. A Roman road crossed the site on its way to the riverside and was lined with buildings, including a massive (20 metre by 10 metre) aisled structure. This period of Worcester's history is now marked inside the building, where a stone-built kiln base from the fourth century AD has been reconstructed under the main staircase, close to where it was found – Worcester's oldest structure preserved inside one of its newest.

34. Worcester Bridge

Crossing Britain's longest river has always been a challenge. The average water flow through Worcester is over 8 million cubic metres daily, and flooding is a regular event. As late as 1400 Worcester was the only bridging point between Bridgnorth and Gloucester, a distance of nearly 60 miles. Elsewhere the river could only be crossed by ferry or ford, and there were several of them in Worcester itself. Since the late twentieth century, Worcester Bridge has been joined by several others: the Carrington road bridge (1985), just south of the city, and the Sabrina (1992) and Diglis (2010) foot and cycle bridges. There has also been a railway bridge across the Severn since 1860 (rebuilt in 1904).

Worcester's medieval bridge was 150 metres upstream from the present one, linking Newport Street on the city side with Tybridge Street on the west bank. It may have had early origins (perhaps even Roman) – a bridge in Worcester needed repairs in 1088. A stone bridge built in 1314 had five pointed arches and a gatehouse at its centre. Its piers were apparently built with Roman iron slag, readily available on the floodplain nearby. Damaged in the Civil War, the bridge was repaired, but it needed replacing by the mid-eighteenth century.

John Gwynn of Shrewsbury, architect of several bridges (including Magdalen Bridge in Oxford), founder member of the Royal Academy and friend of Dr Johnson, was commissioned to design the new bridge. Work started in 1771 and the bridge opened to traffic in 1780. It formed an impressive introduction to the city from the west, with two domed toll houses with urn-shaped chimneys, approached by 'St John's New Road' (now simply New Road) and linked into the city by the Georgian brick terraces of Bridge Street (also by Gwynn, 1788–92, restored as flats in 1981–83). The bridge had five stone arches and there were pedestrian arches under the road at both ends.

Worcester Bridge from South Quay.

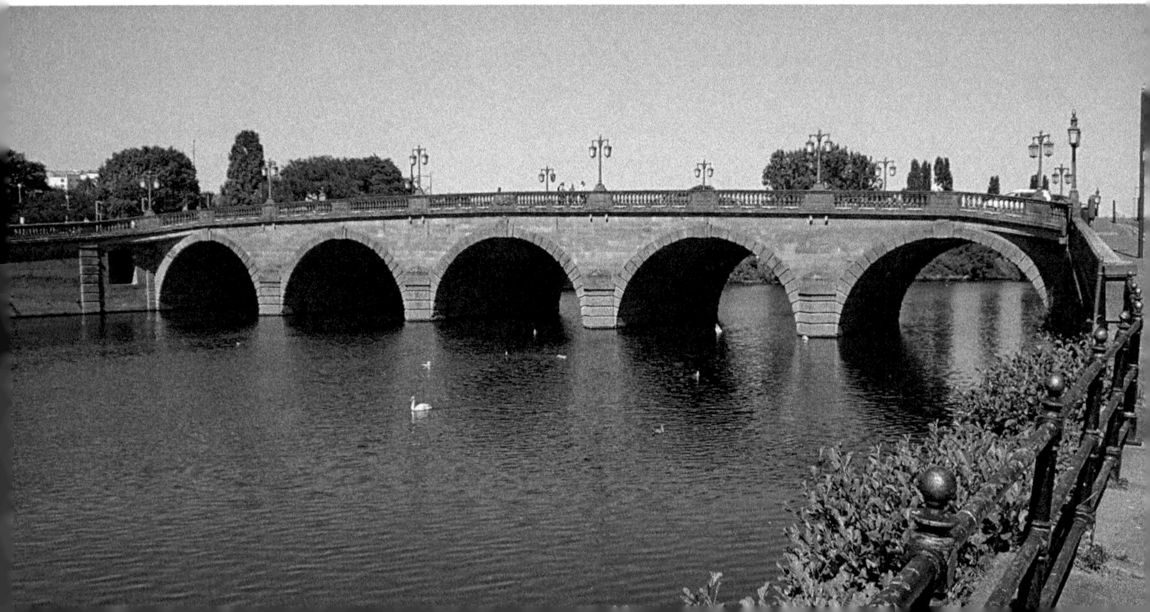

Traffic across the bridge steadily increased, and in 1847 cast-iron footways were added on either side.

In 1931 the toll houses were demolished and new embankments built, and the bridge was widened on both sides. It was reopened by the Prince of Wales in 1932, along with Cripplegate Park. Only some twentieth-century stonework is now visible, except from below, where the arch soffits of the eighteenth-century bridge can still be seen. The design of the widened bridge is similar to the earlier structure, with rusticated stonework and balustrades in Millstone Grit, while the lamp standards (by Hardy and Padmore) strike a more contemporary note.

35. Huntingdon Hall (Countess of Huntingdon's Chapel), Deansway

The Countess of Huntingdon's Connexion is a small group of churches once affiliated to Methodism. There are now around twenty churches in England and a similar number in Sierra Leone. Selina, Countess of Huntingdon, founded the

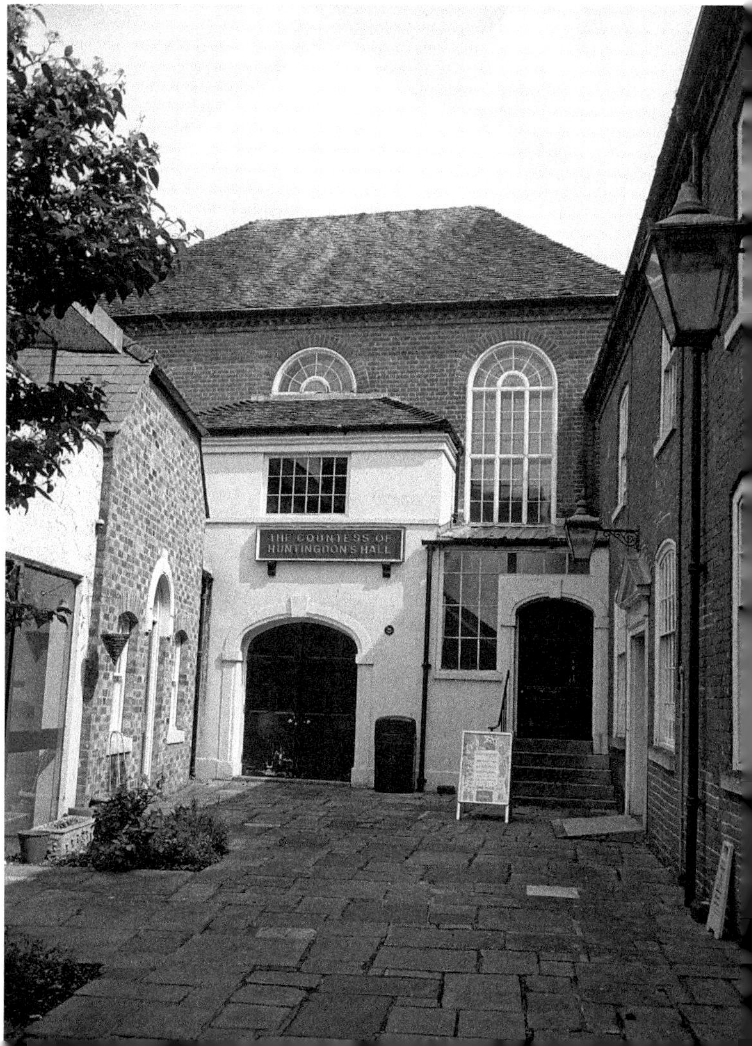

Huntingdon Hall from Deansway.

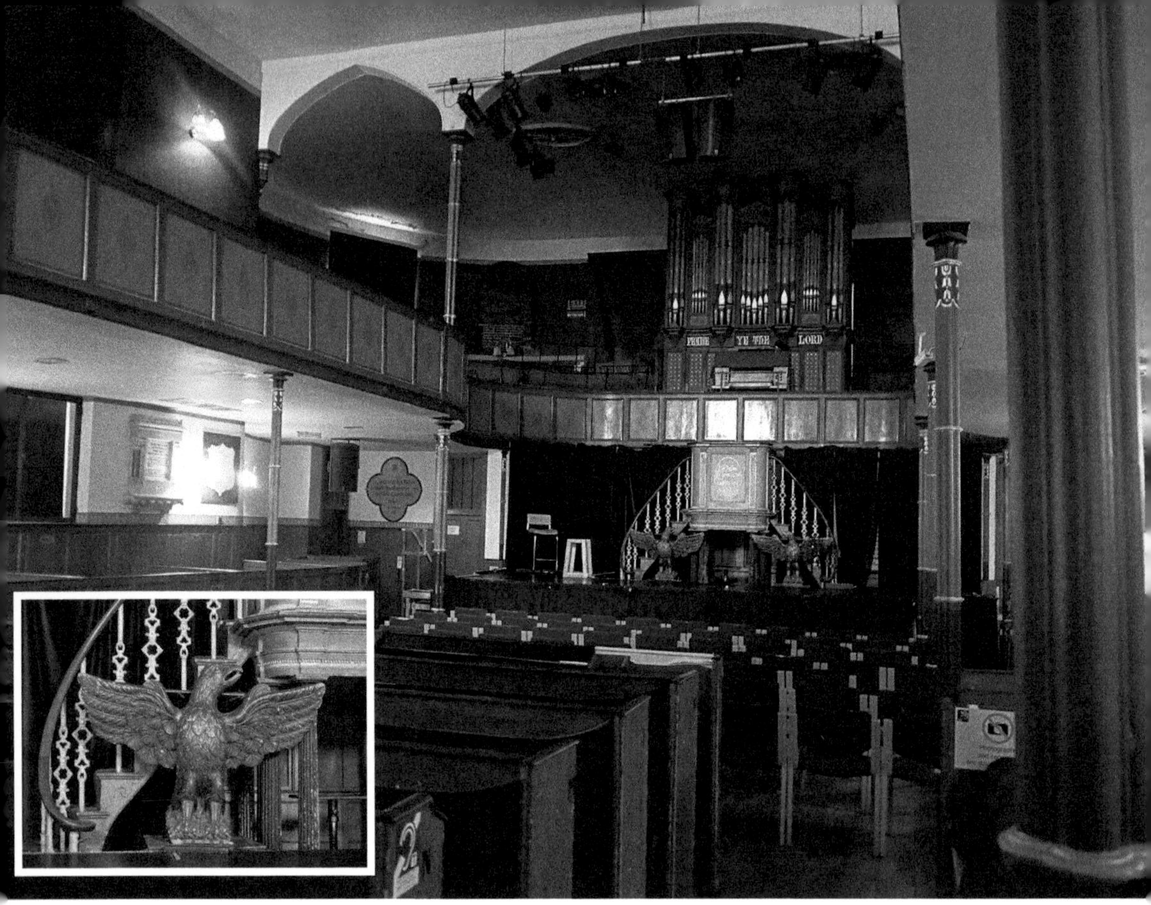

Huntingdon Hall's interior.

Inset: Huntingdon Hall's cast-iron eagle lectern.

first of sixty-four chapels in the 1740s and a Worcester chapel was established in around 1766. A building on this site followed in 1771–73, which was rebuilt in 1804 with a capacity of 1,000, and enlarged in 1815 to hold 2,000. A second church was later built in Lowesmoor (now the Elim Pentecostal Church); the nearest chapel is now at Cradley, Herefordshire.

The complex was squeezed in off Birdport, one of a maze of lanes that were swept away in the mid-twentieth century for the through route of Deansway. It included houses, a manse and schoolrooms, grouped round a small courtyard. All were disused by 1976 and faced with demolition, but were rescued and restored by the City of Worcester Building Preservation Trust, and reopened as a concert hall and music school in 1987. Now surrounded by the Crowngate shopping precinct, which opened in 1992, the chapel forms an atmospheric backdrop to restaurants and cafés.

The 1804 chapel is to the west, brick built and of four bays, with box pews and galleries supported by iron columns. The 1815 eastern range is oval in plan with stuccoed brickwork. It houses an organ, pulpit, cast-iron eagle lecterns and railings. The interior survives largely intact, and provides an atmospheric setting for a wide variety of performances.

36. The Glovers' Needle (St Andrew's Spire)

More even than the cathedral, it is the slender spire of St Andrew's Church that distinguishes the Worcester skyline, especially from the west. The Glovers' Needle is the last upstanding remnant of the church, named for the many glovemakers who lived and worked in the parish. Almost every old building in the parish has gone, demolished in slum clearance programmes in the twentieth century, and replaced by a park, college buildings and car parking. The church was demolished in 1949, the sole victim of proposals that would have seen several of Worcester's city centre churches destroyed. However, the importance of the tower and spire to the city's townscape and skyline was recognised and it, along with fragments of the western aisle walls, was allowed to survive. Wooden bosses from the roof are now in Worcester City Museum and Avoncroft Museum, and some fittings were taken to other churches.

Below left: View of Glovers' Needle from Deansway, with St Alban's and All Saints.

Below right: St Andrew's spire, with St Swithun's and St Martin's in the background. (Samuel and Nathaniel Buck, 1732)

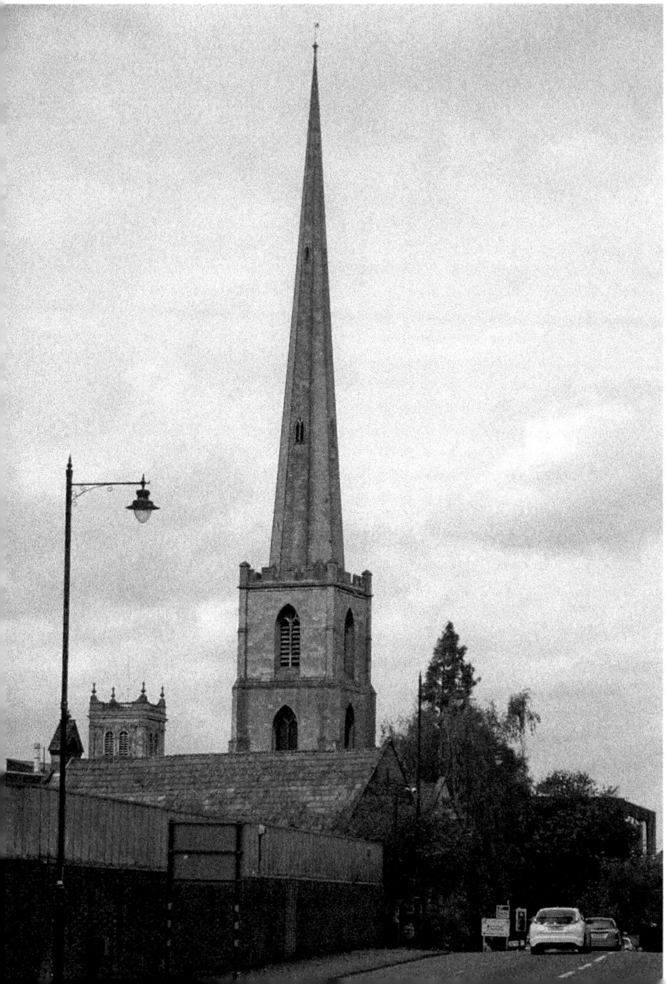

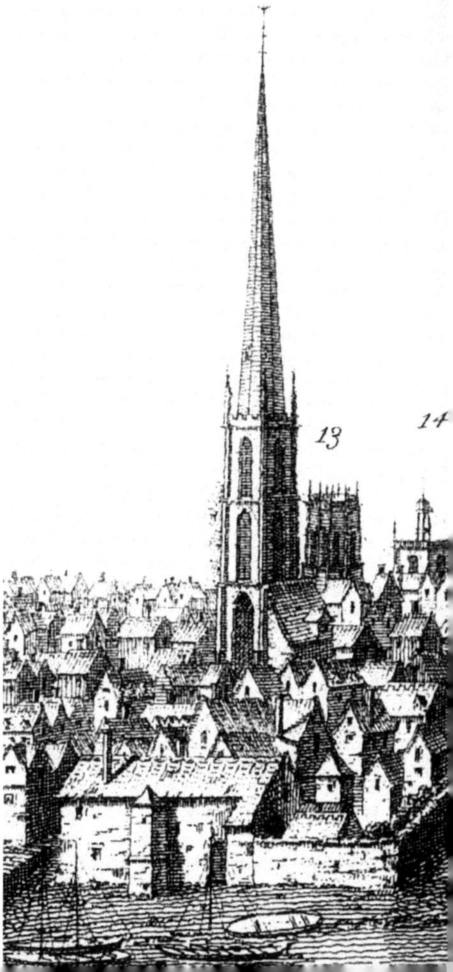

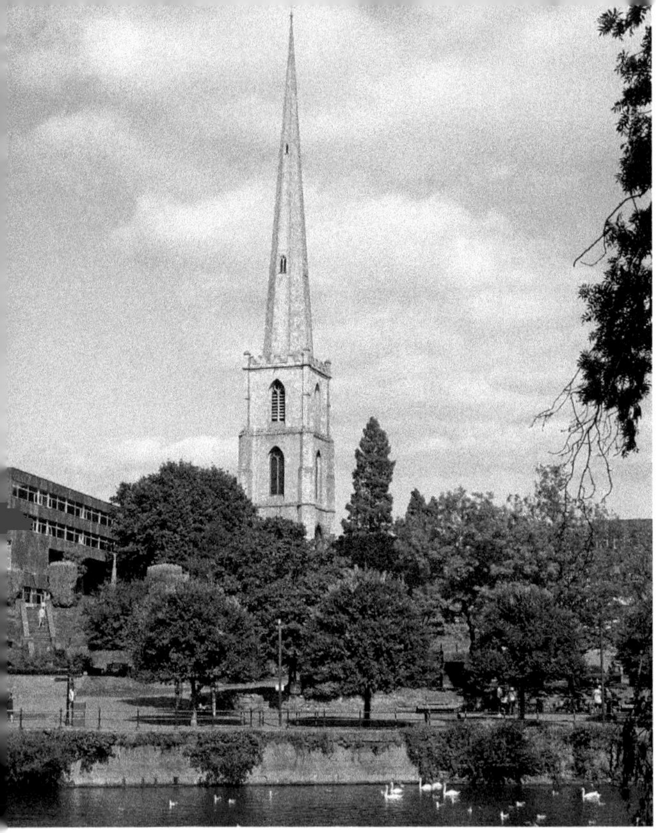

The Glovers' Needle from the river.

The Glovers' Needle is still by some distance the tallest building in Worcester, standing a total of 245 feet (75 metres) high. The tower is 90 feet high and the spire adds an additional 155 feet. It is one of the tallest church steeples in England, and almost three times taller than the church was long (92 feet, 28 metres). The medieval spire, destroyed by lightning in 1733, was shorter (Nash said that it was 134 feet high). The Buck panorama shows it just before its destruction.

The spire was rebuilt in 1751 by Nathaniel Wilkinson, a Worcester stonemason who became known as 'spire-mender' for his work on restoring and rebuilding church spires across the region. In keeping with its mid-eighteenth-century date, the spire was capped with a Corinthian capital. In 1809–12 John Collingwood encased the sandstone tower in Bath stone to match the spire.

The tall spire has presented many challenges over the years. It was damaged by high winds in 1778 and 1799, needing repair both times. In the mid-nineteenth century, the top of the spire was replaced, with the original rebuilt in the churchyard, and it is still a feature in St Andrew's Gardens. When the weathercock on top of the spire was taken down during repairs in 1987 it was found to have a bullet scar. The reason for this is a mystery, but a Worcester resident recalled the air raid of 3 October 1940, when a lone German aircraft bombed the MECO factory in St John's, killing seven people, and machine-gunned the city, and the damage may have been sustained then.

During one restoration, a barber shaved clients on the top platform of the scaffolding while they enjoyed the view, and a painter decorated a porcelain cup.

On another occasion a wine merchant entertained the editor of the *Worcester Chronicle* with a bottle of port at the top.

The medieval tower is finely detailed, with some elaborate masons' marks on the red sandstone. It has a fine lierne vault with thirty-two finely carved stone roof bosses depicting biblical scenes, the apostles and other figures. The vault was endowed by Robert Sutton, a dyer, thought to be the pilgrim to Compostela whose burial, with boots, staff and cockle shell, was excavated in the cathedral in 1986.

The medieval church was short and wide, with aisles that extended westwards to clasp the tower. This layout ensured that there was room for a processional way all round the church, within the churchyard, consecrated for burials in 1635.

Recently the tower parapet was colonised by a pair of peregrine falcons who have raised several chicks here, watched by thousands over the internet.

37. The Old Palace

The Old Palace is one of Worcester's best-kept secrets. Towards the busy traffic route of Deansway the palace and its extensive gardens are largely hidden by high stone and brick walls, and only from the riverside does it make a strong visual impression.

There has been a bishop's palace here since late Saxon times, and Bishop Wulfstan undertook a major building campaign. His palace is thought to have

Old Palace's baroque east front.

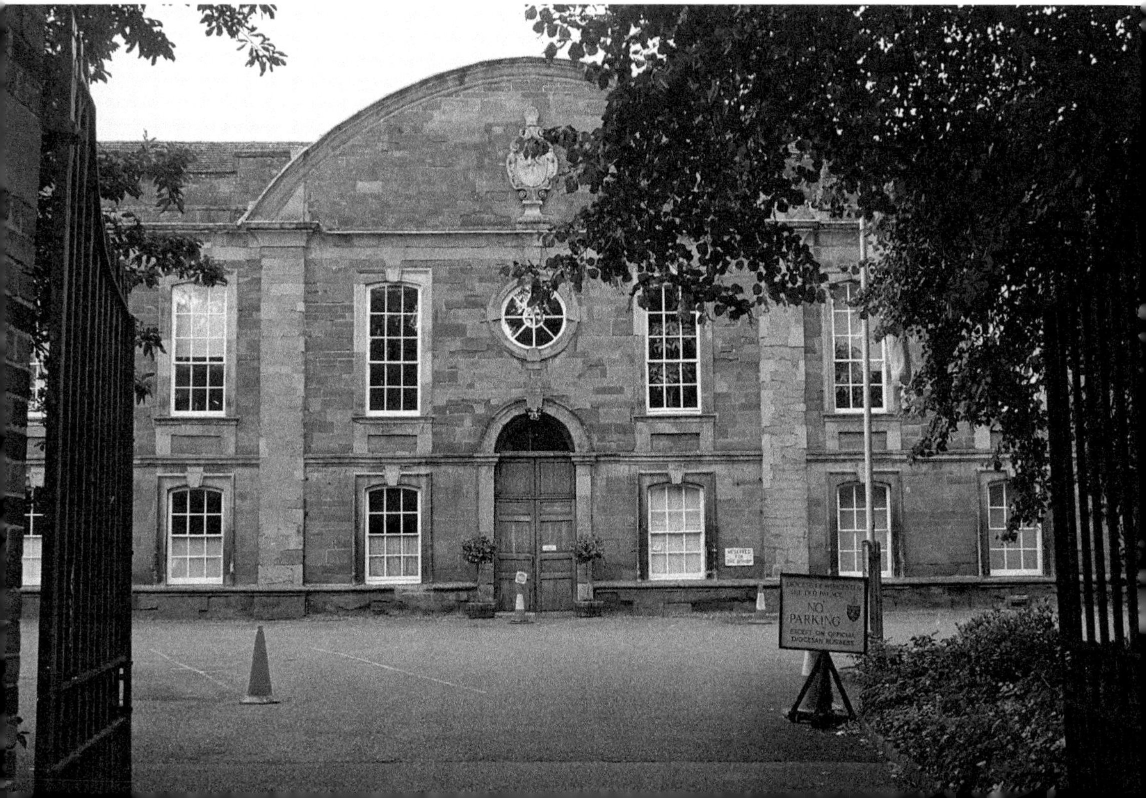

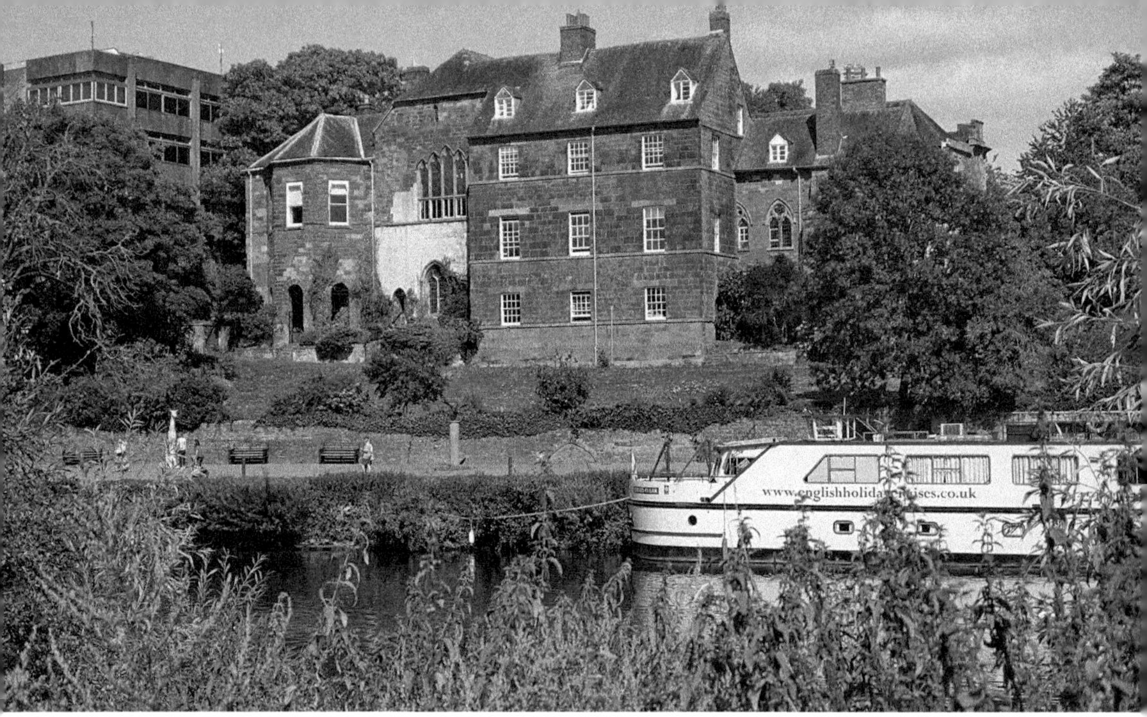

Above: The Old Palace from the riverside.

Below: The thirteenth-century Great Hall, Old Palace.

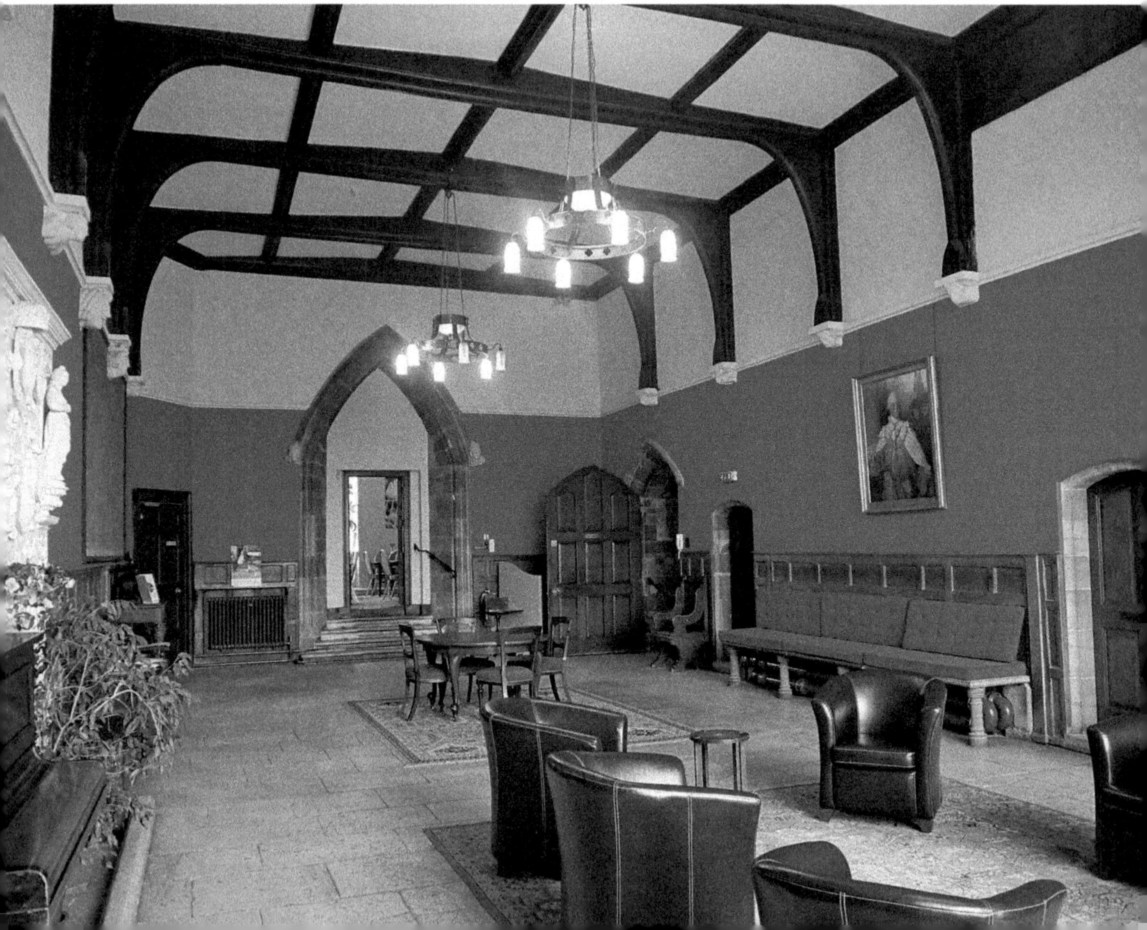

had a large great hall, probably aisled. However, nothing is known to survive from this early date. The oldest visible fabric is early thirteenth century, including rib-vaulted undercrofts and part of the south wall with a blocked Norman window. Bishop Giffard was granted licence to crenellate in 1271. The vaulted 'Abbot's Kitchen' and Great Hall survive from his rebuilding, though the latter was extensively remodelled in the fifteenth century and later and has an impressive seventeenth-century fireplace. Of the medieval bishop's chapel, only the chancel survives, which was was reordered and realigned north–south in the 1560s.

The loose plan of the medieval palace buildings, partly on the slope down to the river, was given some unity by Bishop Hough's new east front of 1719–23. The two-storey façade, with its low battlements, segmental pediment and oculus window, was designed by William Smith. Colvin described it as 'bumbling Baroque'. Other alterations in the eighteenth century included a three-and-a-half-storey block facing the river and Bishop Hurd's drawing room with its large bay window.

Four monarchs have stayed here: Elizabeth I (1575), Charles I (1644), James II (1687) and George III (1788). No bishop has lived in the palace since 1846, when the building was sold to the dean and chapter of the cathedral. It was used as the Deanery for a century. It now houses the offices of the diocese of Worcester, and the main rooms are also used for events.

38. Kays Building, The Tything

For over two centuries Kays was one of Worcester's main employers, growing from a small shop by St Swithun's Church into one of Britain's largest mail order catalogue businesses, long before the arrival of the internet.

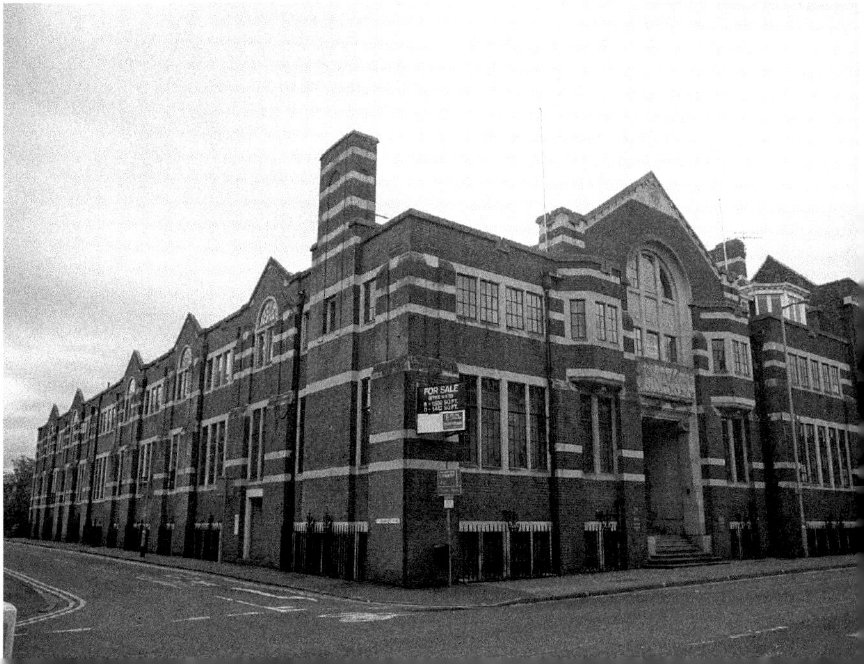

The Kays building.

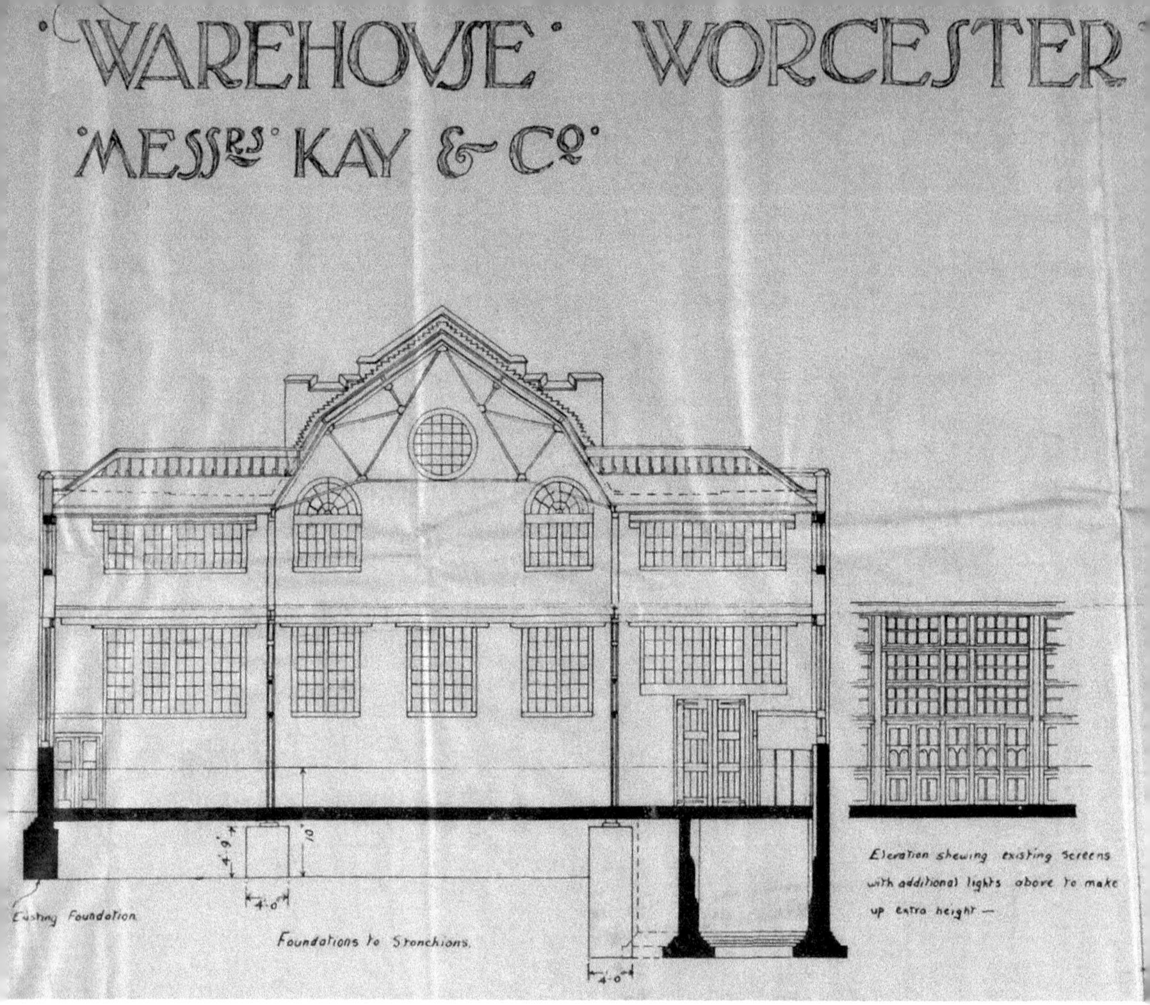

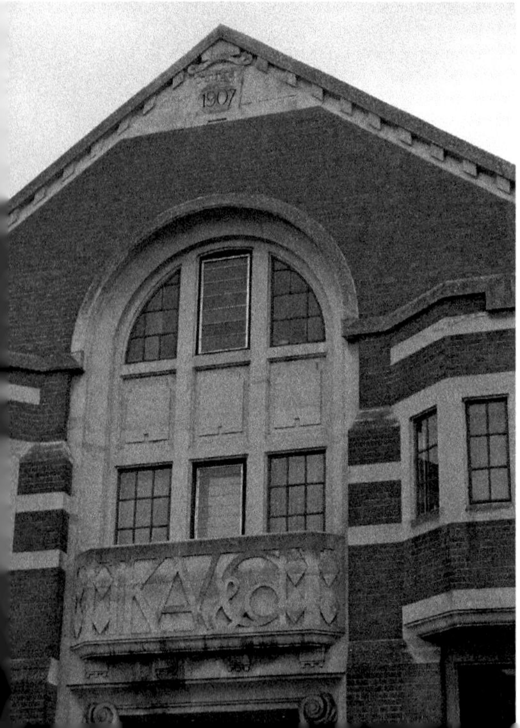

Above: A Cross-section of the Kays building, 1907. (John Simpson and Maxwell Ayrton, Worcester City Archives)

Left: Detail of the Kays building's main façade.

The building in The Tything, which still bears their name, dates from the beginning of the twentieth century, and provided offices and a warehouse. It is a bold composition in a simplified modern style by J. W. Simpson and Maxwell Ayrton (1907, extended in 1914), throwing off late Victorian and Edwardian convention, brick built with stone banding and metal-framed windows. The asymmetrical elevation to The Tything is particularly striking, with its oriel windows and bold lettering (Kay & Co.), and it sits happily in the largely Georgian streetscape. The long façade to the side, along St Oswalds Road, is more subtle but equally successful, with finely detailed pilaster buttresses, projecting bays, a great variety of windows and many gables.

Ten years earlier, Simpson had worked in Worcester on the Victoria Institute, then in partnership with Milner Allen, and in a much more traditional style. Simpson and Maxwell Ayrton also designed an elegant pavilion for Kays sports ground near here, now sadly demolished. Maxwell Ayrton went on to design the twin towers of Wembley Stadium.

Kays' later buildings were more conventional including a neo-Georgian building several doors down in The Tything, and a massive 1970s warehouse on the western edge of Worcester (now demolished), which prefigured the 'fulfilment centres' of Amazon and the other internet giants.

The Kays building was converted into apartments in the early twenty-first century.

39. Britannia Square

At the beginning of the nineteenth century many of Worcester's middle classes deserted the overcrowded and insanitary city centre for leafy suburbs, mostly on the hills to the east – Lansdowne Crescent, Green Hill and Lark Hill are typical. Britannia Square was the earliest and finest of these. Plots were laid out in the Windmill Field (just next to the medieval Tything suburb) from around 1815. One thing nearly all these Regency developments had in common was that

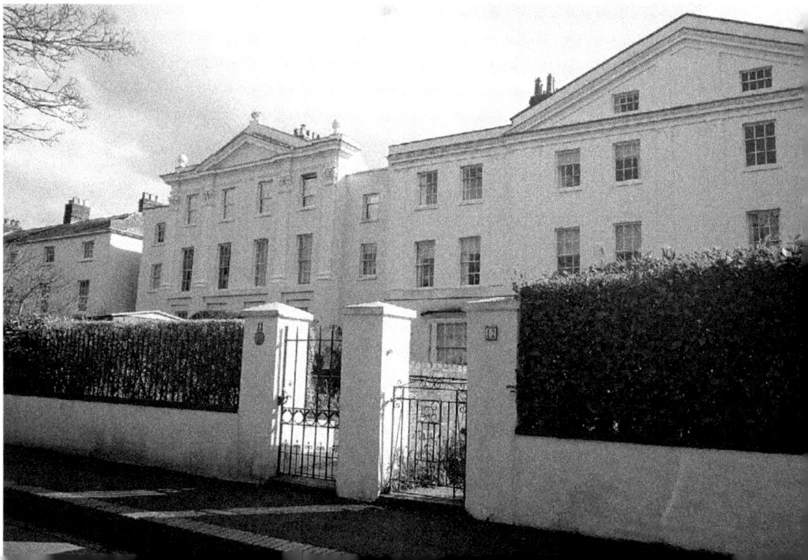

Houses on the south side of Britannia Square.

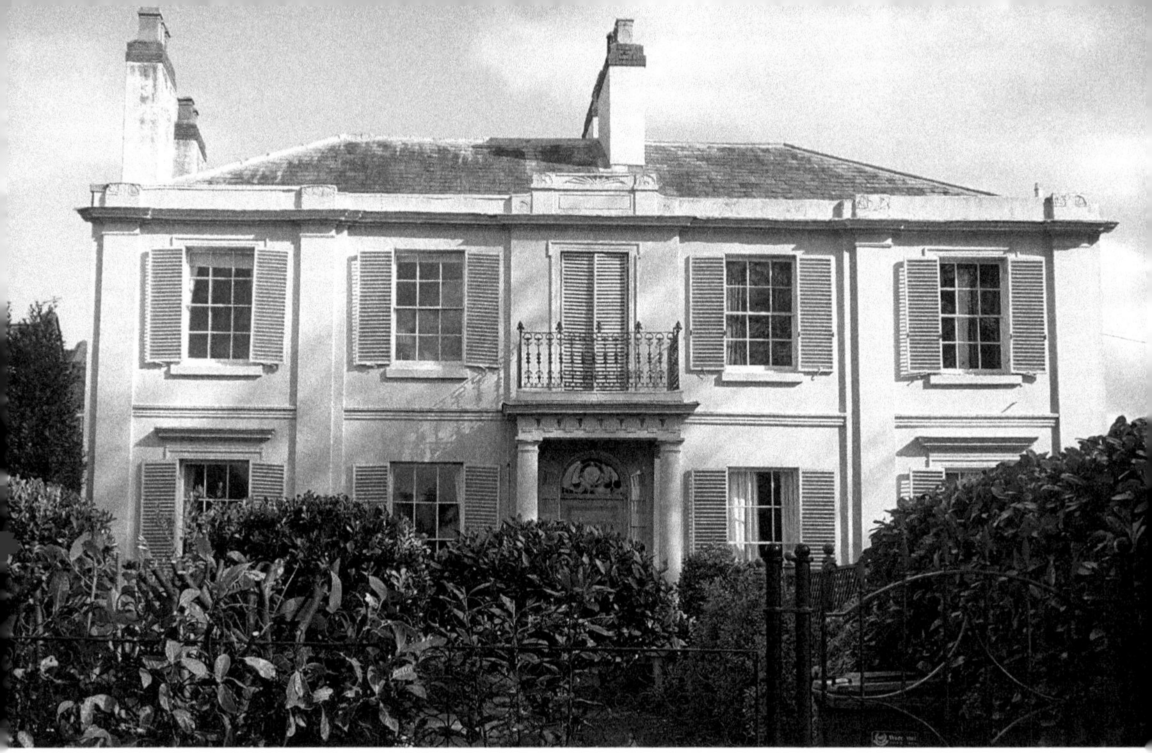

A house on the east side of Britannia Square.

building plots were sold with a design code stipulating location, height, and the white stucco finish; it is rare for two houses to be the same.

The Britannia Square houses were built very much for show, with a small number of large reception rooms. The plots were not large, and the houses were to be built close to the back, giving the maximum space for an impressive garden approach to the front door. To the rear were kitchens, outhouses and servants quarters, and the back lanes mostly gave onto lower-class housing; indeed, the prison was very close on the south side.

Development of the south and east sides of the square was well underway by 1822, and the west side from 1826. The north side was the last to be built up in the 1830s. On the north, west and east sides, the houses were mostly detached, while several on the south side formed a terrace. Here, Albion House is enhanced with pilasters and a grand pediment.

Springfield (now a school), in the centre of the square, was built around 1830. In 1829, excavation for foundations revealed parts of a Roman building, perhaps a villa, and further Roman remains have been found in the area more recently, including a small fragment of a mosaic from a bathhouse.

To the north of Britannia Square other less grand developments grew up. In Albany Terrace there are stucco terraces from the 1820s–30s. No. 4 is in a mixed Egyptian and Greek style with a chimney shaped as a stylised crocus. York Place (1831–35) is made up of continuous terraces in red brick. Built for the 'artisan class', these houses are now highly sought after.

40. St George's Church, Barbourne

St George's Church is the centrepiece of the elongated square named after it. Most of the houses in St George's Square are from the 1830s and built in red brick. The church of 1893–95 was designed by Aston Webb, and is 'a key work of his early and best period' (Pevsner). It replaced a small chapel of ease to Claines, which was built in 1830.

Webb had family connections with Worcestershire: his wife was the daughter of Edward Evans, one of the founders of the Hill, Evans vinegar works in Lowesmoor. He gained a lot of his early commissions in the county including church restorations (All Saints, St Helen's and Claines) and vicarages. Among his other buildings in Worcester are the Queen Elizabeth Almshouses and the Old Quilt Factory in Angel Place (formerly a Sunday school). Later in his career he became the architect of choice for the late Imperial bombast of the Victoria and Albert Museum and the grand ceremonial route of The Mall, including the Admiralty Arch and the refronting of Buckingham Palace. Webb worked there with Worcester's Sir Thomas Brock to create the imposing Victoria Memorial, which stands in front of the palace.

Both outside and in, St George's is built of red brick, with stone dressings used quite sparingly. The west front is marked by a massive arch over the doorway, and topped with two turrets with spirelets. Very few furnishings were retained from the earlier church; most are contemporary with the building, with few later alterations. There are some very good Arts and Crafts and art nouveau features, and the organ case has painted decoration with Pre-Raphaelite figures.

St George's Square.

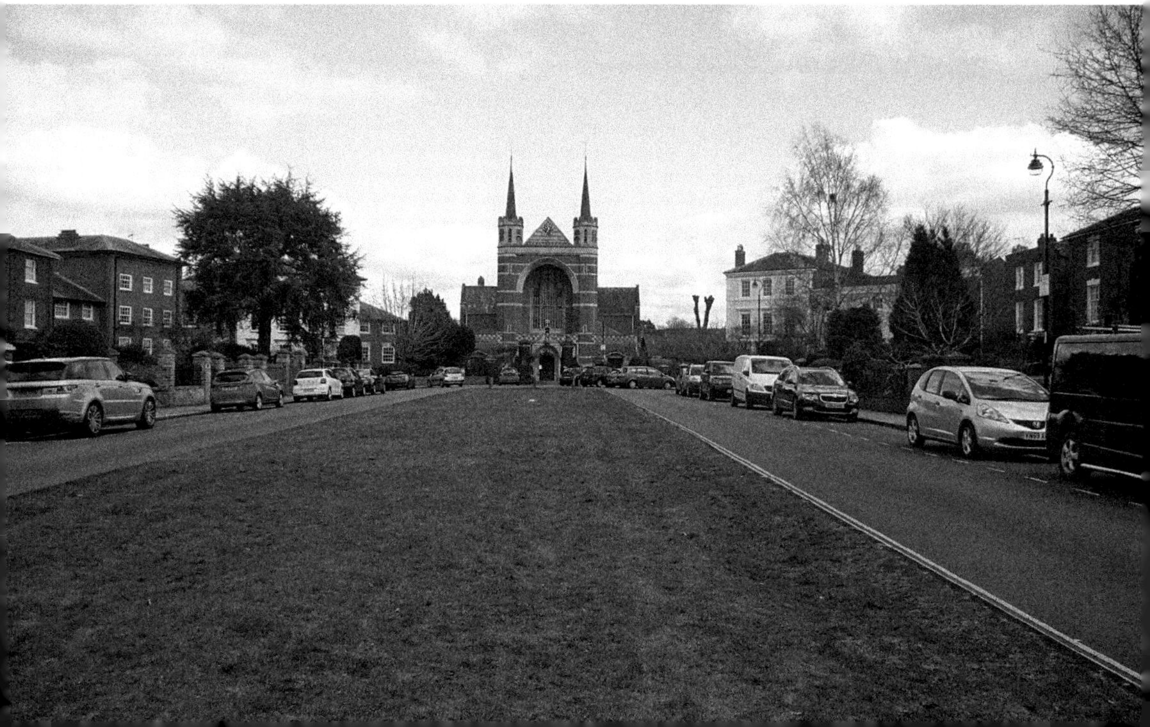

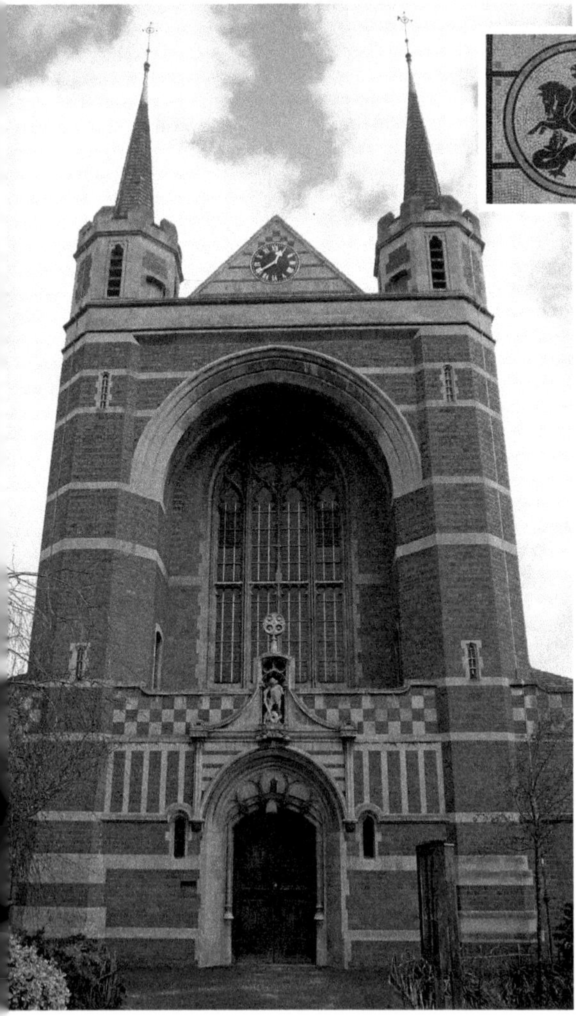

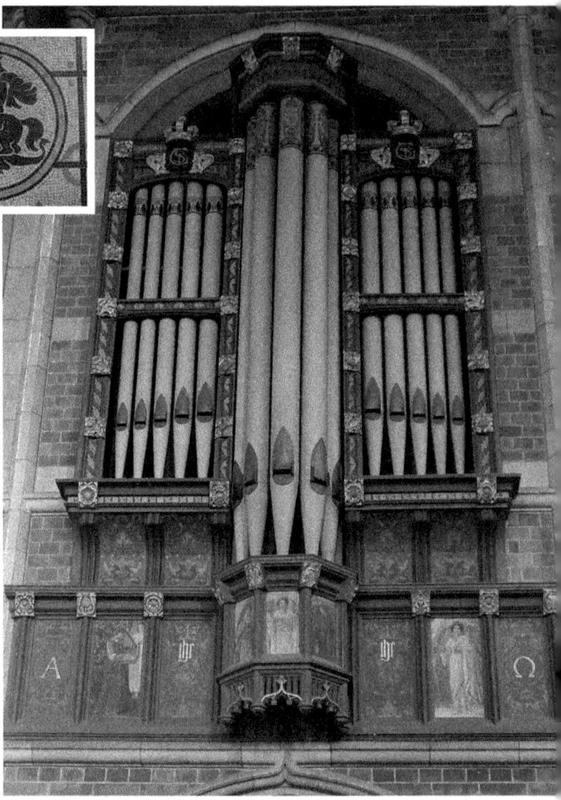

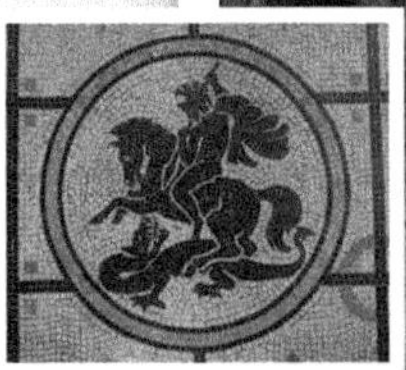

Above: Painted organ case.

Left: The west front of St George's Church, Barbourne.

Inset: Aston Webb's mosaic of St George and the dragon.

41. Gheluvelt Park and Memorial Arch

Plans for a park here had been considered before the First World War and were given impetus by the decision to dedicate it as a war memorial. It occupies the site of Barbourne House and its grounds in the valley of the Barbourne Brook. An earlier house here was used as a Parliamentary headquarters during the Civil War.

Gheluvelt Park is named after the Worcestershire Regiment's heroic action at the Belgian village of Geluveld, just east of Ypres. This took place on 31 October 1914 during the First Battle of Ypres. Thirty-four died and 153 were wounded during a counter-attack, disrupting a German offensive that was likely to have breached the British line. The park and its various buildings – archway, bandstand and houses for disabled ex-servicemen – now stand as a memorial to those who fought at Gheluvelt.

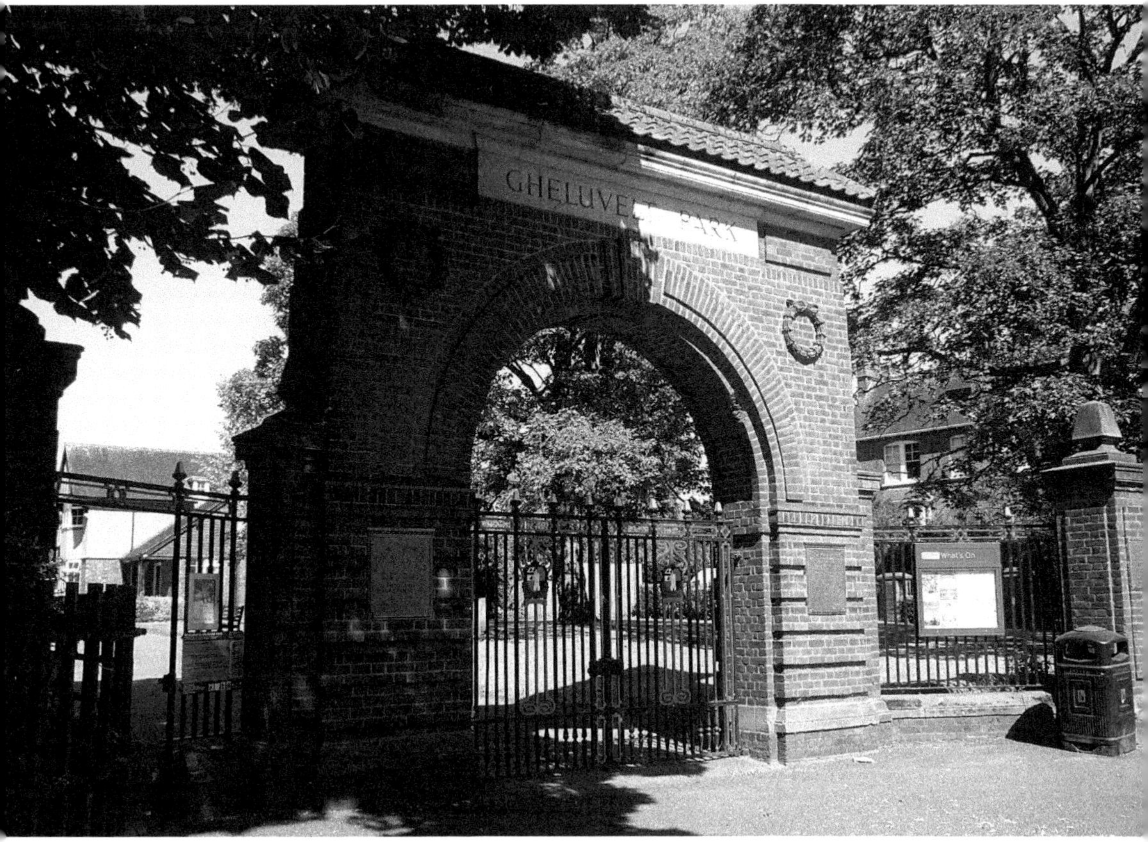

Above: The entrance archway to Gheluvelt Park.

Right: The bandstand in Gheluvelt Park.

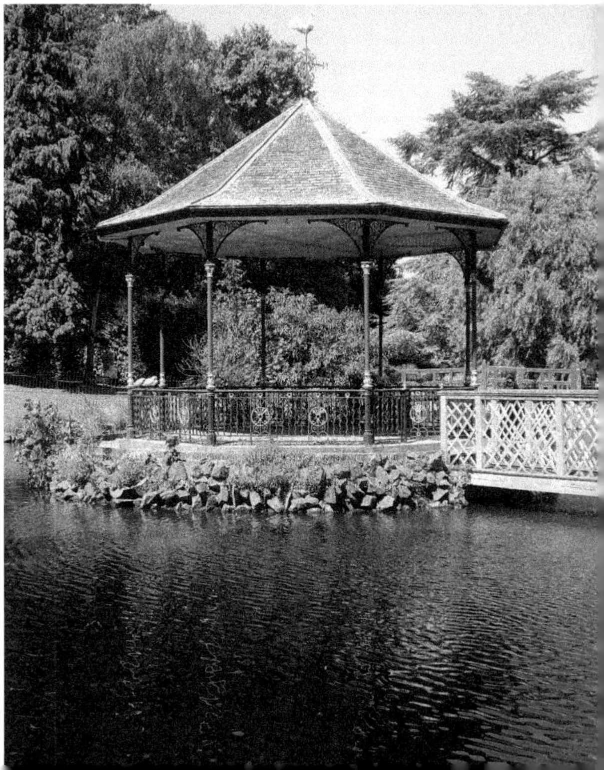

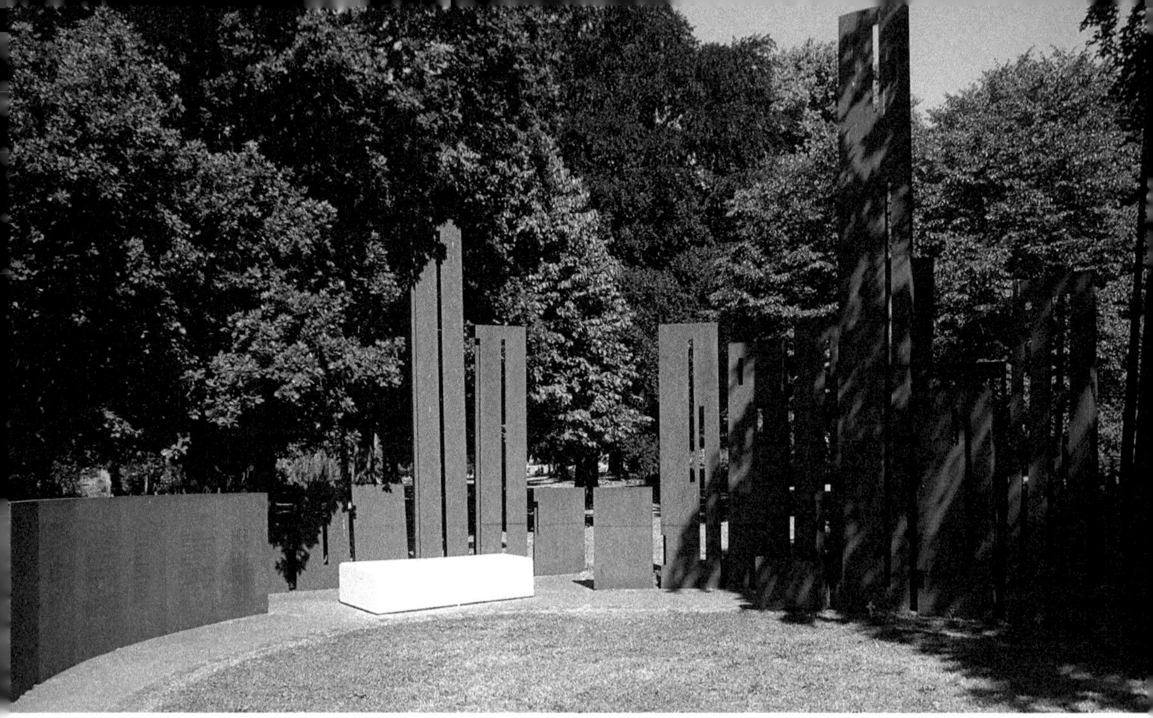

The First World War memorial in Gheluvelt Park.

Planning for the new park started in earnest in 1918 and it was opened on 17 June 1922 by Field Marshal John French, who said that 'on that day the 2nd Worcesters saved the British Empire'. The park was laid out to the designs of Alfred Hill Parker, who also designed the buildings, but was incomplete when the opening took place. The ex-servicemen's houses had been built in 1919–20, but park layout was still underway in 1923–24.

The twelve houses face a roadway along the top of the park. They are maintained by Haig Homes. Apart from a detached bungalow, the 'picturesque vernacular' houses are in groups of two or three, of red brick, with pebble-dash and render and hipped tiled roofs. The vernacular theme is accentuated by tile hanging and applied timber framing.

The cast-iron bandstand (1923) is unusually sited on an artificial island in the middle of the Barbourne Brook, reached by a drawbridge. This is the only surviving bandstand in any of Worcester's parks, and is regularly used in the summer. The park's most distinctive feature is the entrance archway (1924). Again designed by Hill Parker, the round-headed brick arch has stone dressings, a pantiled cap, iron gates and railings, and decorative metal panels showing the city's arms.

As part of the refurbishment of the park in 2010, a new war memorial was created (designed by Plincke). This is a curved setting of slabs of corten steel (which has a stable rusted surface layer). The heights of the slabs relate to British Empire war casualties by two-monthly periods. A panel is inscribed with the names of the fallen of the Worcestershire Regiment in the First World War.

In 2000, with the closure of the adjacent waterworks, the park was extended westwards to the Severn. The three conjoined pumping houses by Hawksley

(1857–58, 1868) and Caink (1901–02) are now an environmental education centre and café. Next to the Barbourne Brook is the restored base of a circular water tower of around 1770, which fed water to the city centre by gravity.

In 2015, Gheluvelt Park was registered as a historic park and garden and the buildings listed.

42. Northwick Cinema, Ombersley Road

The Northwick is by far the finest of Worcester's early twentieth-century cinemas. It was built not in the city centre, but on the edge of Barbourne, far out in the suburbs. In the 1930s Worcester was expanding rapidly northwards, and a ready audience must have seemed guaranteed, though the Second World War was underway only a year after it was built. The plain brick exterior in art deco style is characterised by the bold vertical fin bearing the cinema's name, but otherwise gives no hint of the cinema's dramatic interior. The architect for the building was C. Edmund Wilford of Leicester (1938), and the interior had been as designed by John Alexander a couple of years earlier in 1936. Alexander was at the time one of the best-known cinema designers, but very little of his work survives; this is now the best example to be seen.

Northwick cinema.

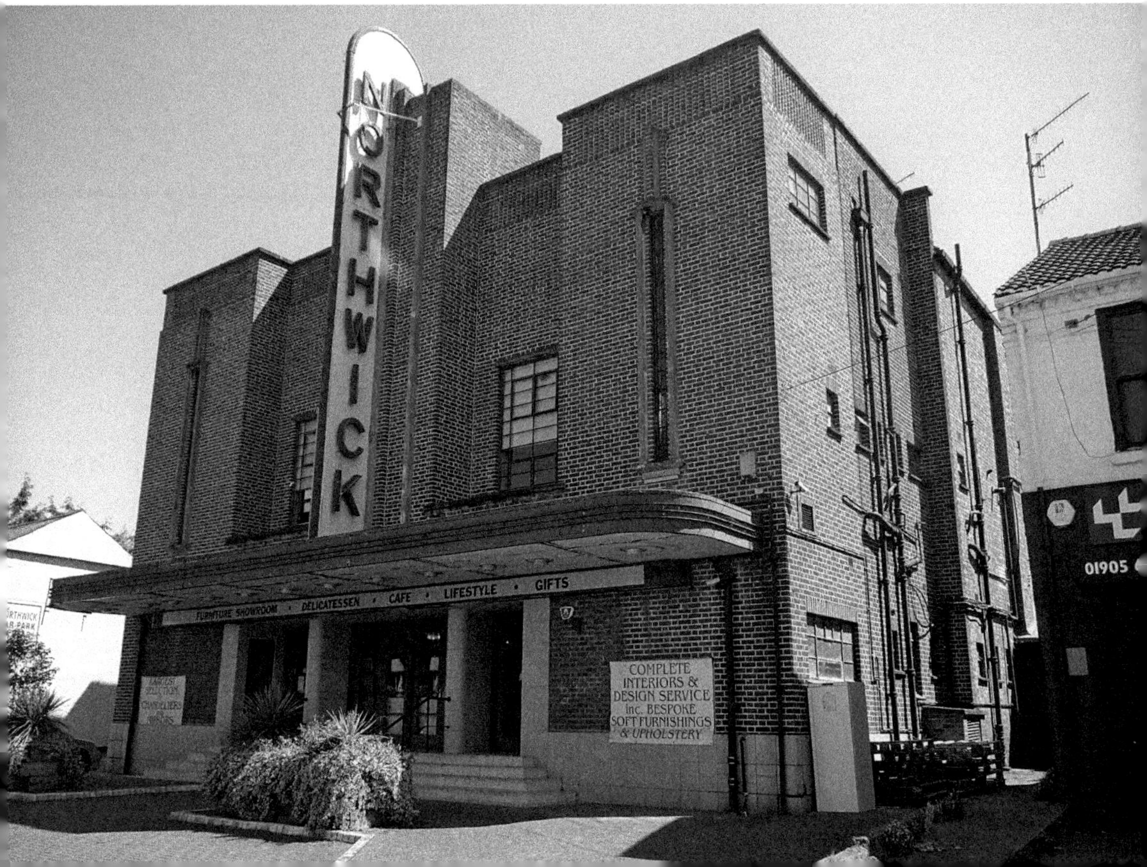

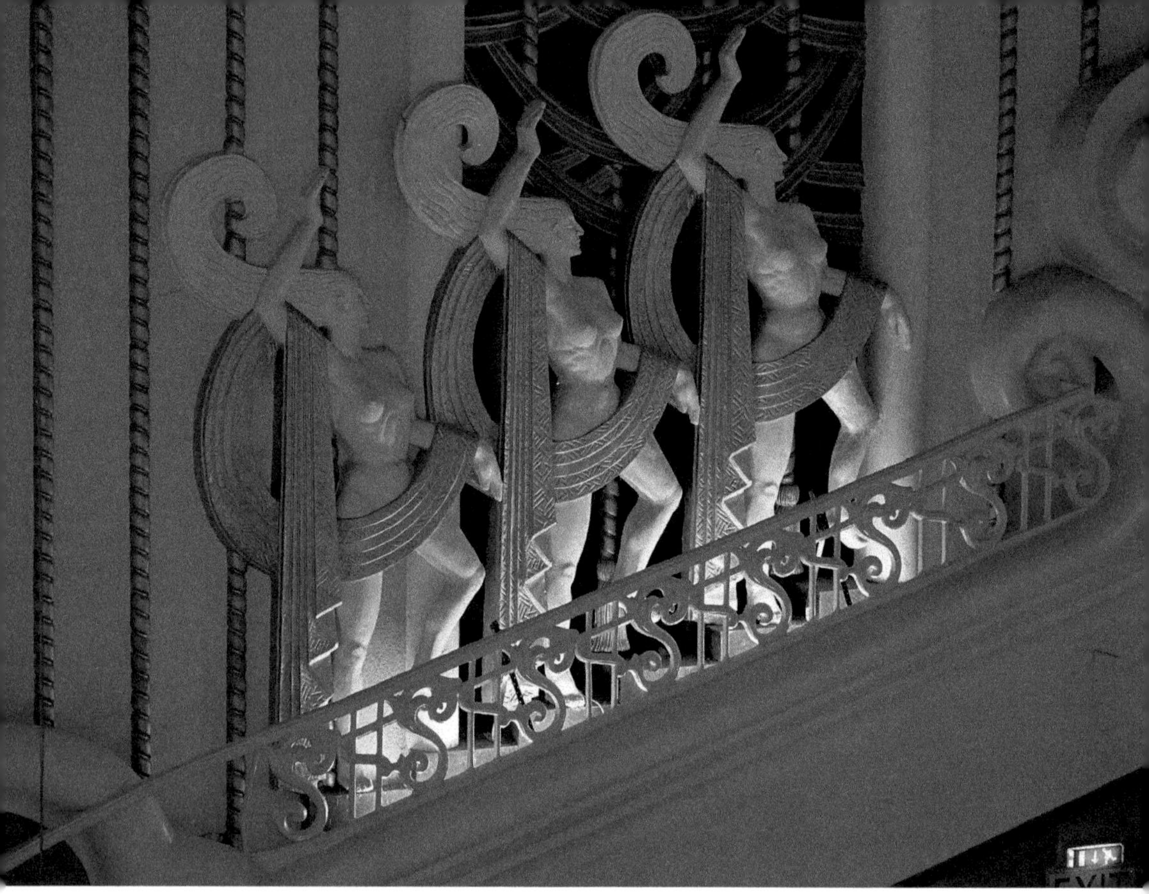

Detail of John Alexander's auditorium decoration.

Although the seats have gone, the latest use of the cinema as an upmarket furniture and lighting shop means that visitors have access to the auditorium and can easily appreciate the splendour of the decoration. Many minor features can be sought out by art deco fans including ashtrays, lights and door fittings, and plaster and stencil decoration is widespread. However, it is the figures either side of the proscenium arch that are the most dramatic: groups of three half-clothed female figures posed with stylised hair and drapery.

The influence of these artworks has been surprisingly far-reaching. The artist Kasia Charko describes visiting the Northwick regularly as a child in the 1960s, and was inspired to produce hundreds of art deco images and designs for the Biba department store, before becoming one of Canada's leading children's book illustrators.

43. Shrub Hill Station and Waiting Rooms

The Oxford, Worcester & Wolverhampton Railway reached Worcester in 1850, though the present Shrub Hill station dates mainly from 1863–64, when the line had been taken over by the Great Western Railway. With its porte-cochere and

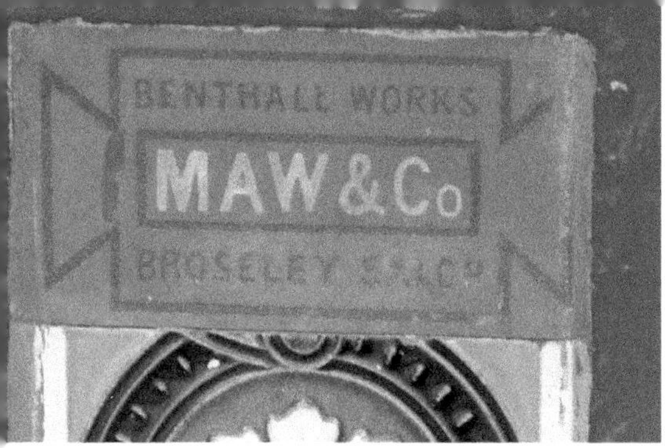

Above: Maw & Co. company tile.

Right: Shrub Hill station's waiting room on platform two.

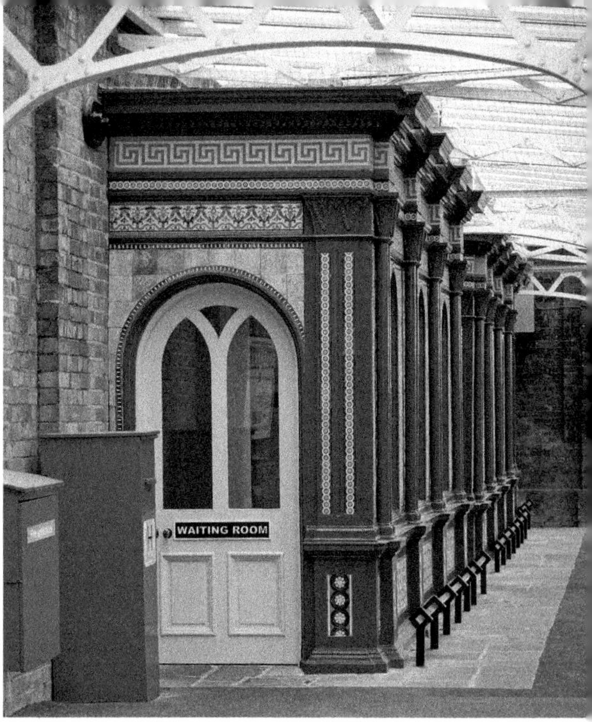

Detail of cast-iron and tile decoration.

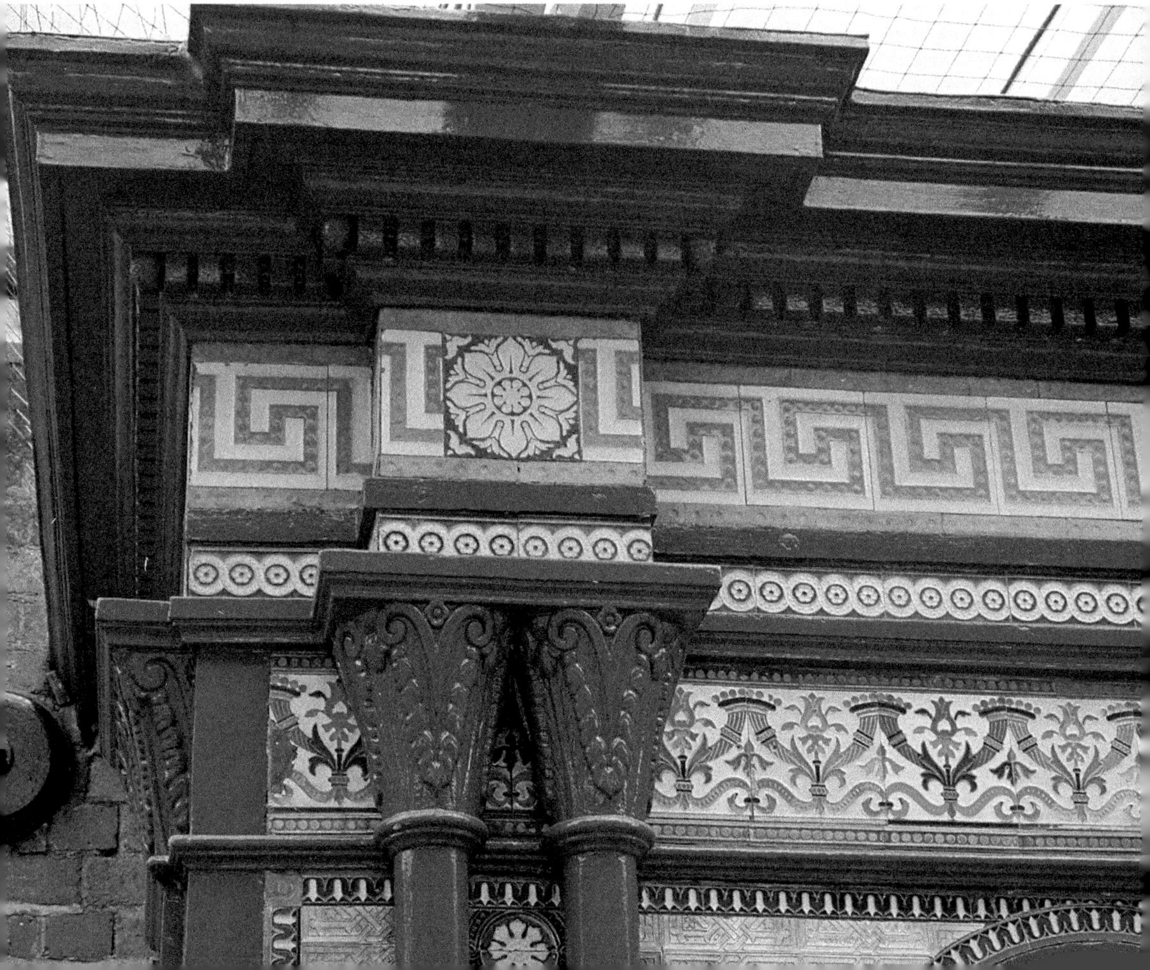

long façade towards the city, it is an impressive gateway to Worcester, though less imposing within since the glazed canopies were removed in 1936.

The highly ornate waiting rooms on the up platform come as a surprise. Probably contemporary with the rebuilding of the station in the 1860s, the structure is a showcase for the industrial arts, specifically the tile makers Maw & Co. of Broseley, who had recently moved from Worcester in 1852, and the more local iron founders of the Vulcan Ironworks, Shrub Hill Road, which was founded in 1857. The signatures of both makers, in their respective materials, are prominent on the façade.

The waiting rooms are framed in cast iron and decorated with relief-moulded shafts with acanthus capitals and an elaborately moulded cornice. Wooden windows and doors are set into the iron frame. The tiles are both relief decorated and highly coloured (using the cuenca technique where the different colours are separated by raised clay borders), and cover virtually all the available space on the outside. The style is eclectic, with a Greek key pattern frieze vying with Moorish elements reminiscent of Granada. Initially, the structure consisted of two three-bay rooms separated by a small lobby. The southernmost bay was added in the 1870s and is a quite plain design of conventional brick and stucco construction. Inside, the waiting room is, disappointingly, quite undecorated, with characteristic plain Great Western benches.

The early history of this ornate waiting room is unknown. It has been suggested that it was an exhibition piece, and that it could have been moved here from elsewhere, though there is no evidence for this. After years of neglect it has been repaired with help from the Railway Heritage Trust.

44. Shrub Hill Engine Works

The opening of Shrub Hill station sparked the industrial development of the surrounding area. Full advantage was taken of the opportunity to link into the railway, and signs of the extensive rail system that linked the buildings can be seen everywhere: tracks, tunnels and oddly shaped buildings with angled corners to allow the trains to pass. On Shrub Hill Road, road traffic on a level crossing was controlled by a semaphore signal, which is now in the National Railway Museum in York. One branch line ran in a tunnel below the engine works building and under Shrub Hill Road.

The Worcester Engine Works opened in 1864 in buildings designed by Thomas Dickson. Sadly engine building did not prove a success in Worcester, and with the Great Western focusing on their own works at Swindon, the renamed West Central Wagon Works closed in 1871. The building found a new but short-lived use in 1882 when its wide interior spaces amply housed the Worcestershire Exhibition. Heenan Froude, an engineering company, occupied it from 1903–84, and it is now split into multiple uses.

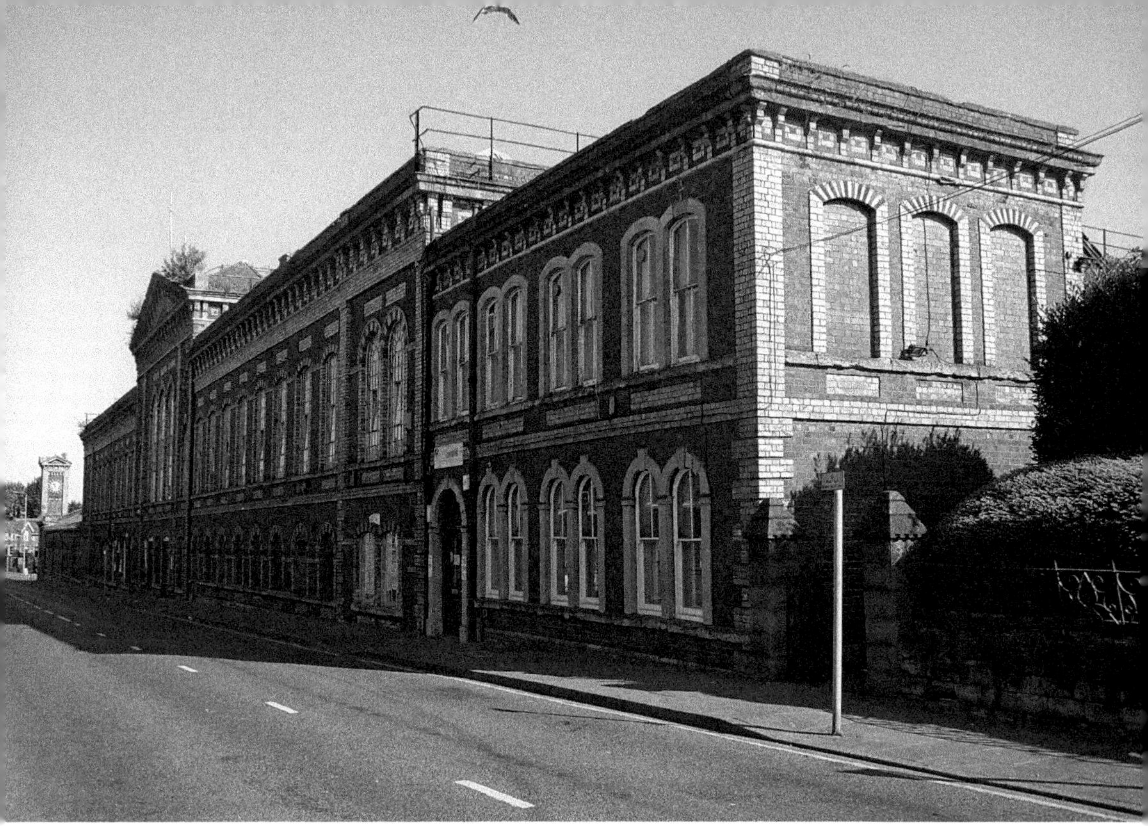

Above: The engine works from Shrub Hill Road.

Right: The polychrome brick tower.

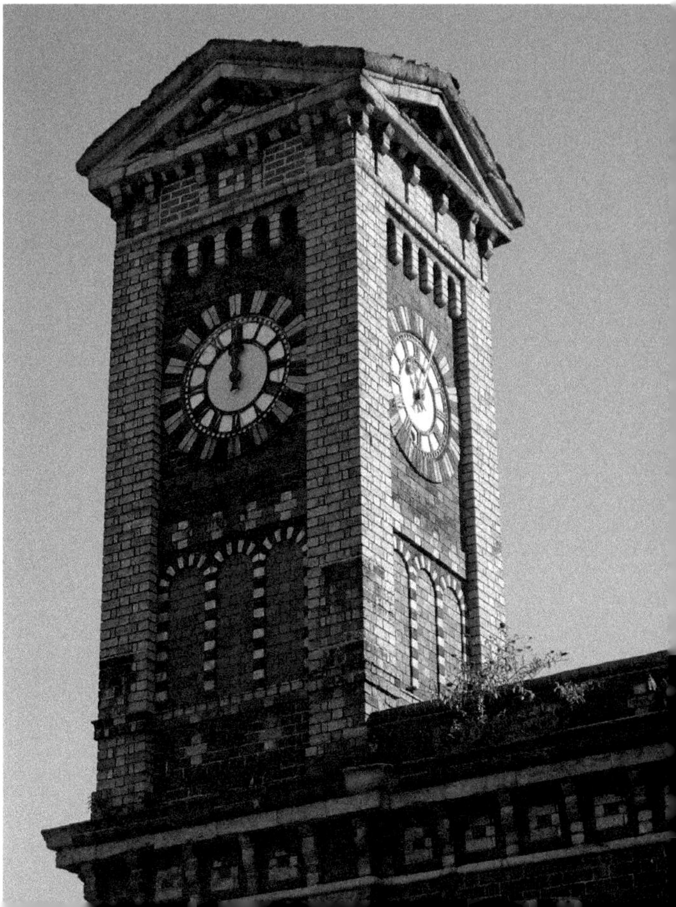

The display of polychrome brickwork will be familiar from other buildings in Worcester and is used here on the largest scale. The façade runs for a total of thirty-seven bays from an Italianate clock tower on the corner of Tolladine Road up to a gateway, which marks the site of Holy Trinity Church. The centre has an impressive pediment facing the city.

45. St Nicholas, Warndon

Warndon church has retained the character that many small Worcestershire parish churches would have had before Victorian restoration. Its village is long deserted apart from the early seventeenth-century Warndon Court, the county's earliest brick house, whose moat also encloses the church. The church has seen a new lease of life with the development, since 1990, of Worcester's suburb of Warndon Villages, but the houses and industrial estates have largely been kept at a distance, conserving a semi-rural atmosphere.

The church retains evidence of many periods, from the round-headed Norman north and south doorways onwards. Most of the windows are Perpendicular in style, and the little timber porch may date from the fifteenth century. From the outside the most striking feature is the close-studded timber tower, one of five in Worcestershire and dating from around 1500. In the latest restoration (1991–92) the outside of the church was rendered and painted white.

St Nicholas, Warndon, from the north.

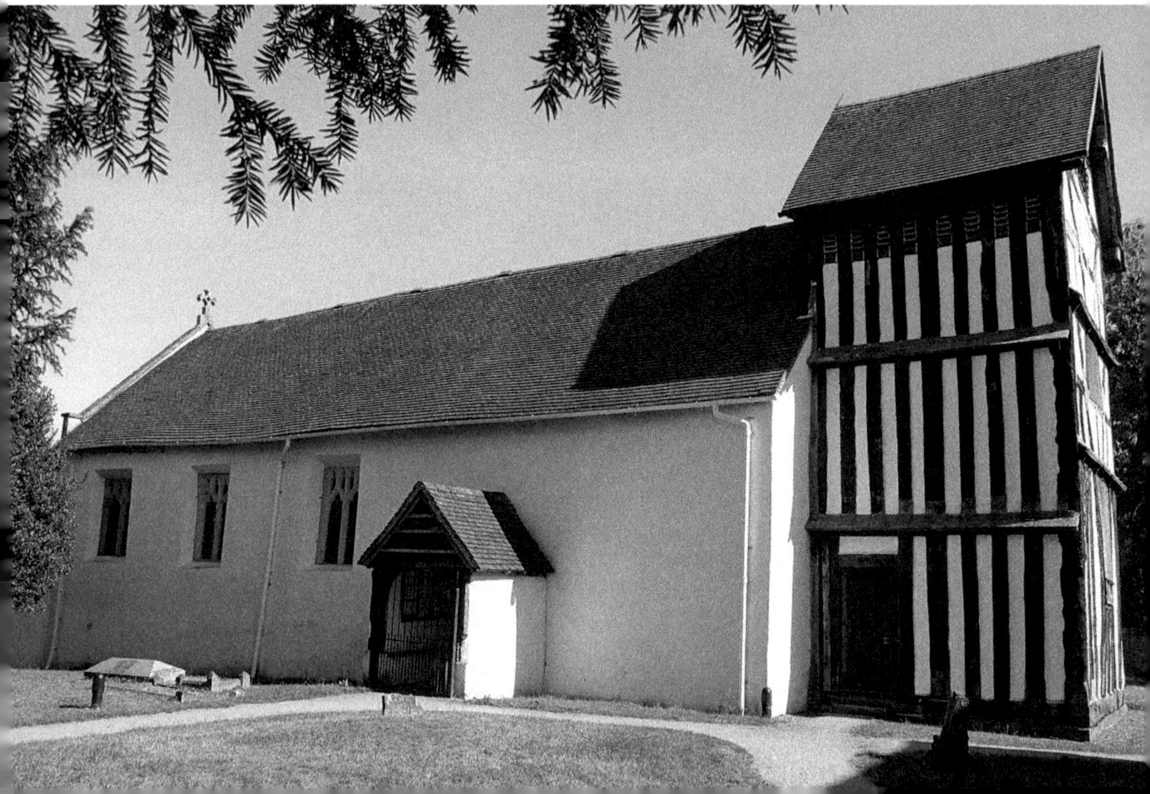

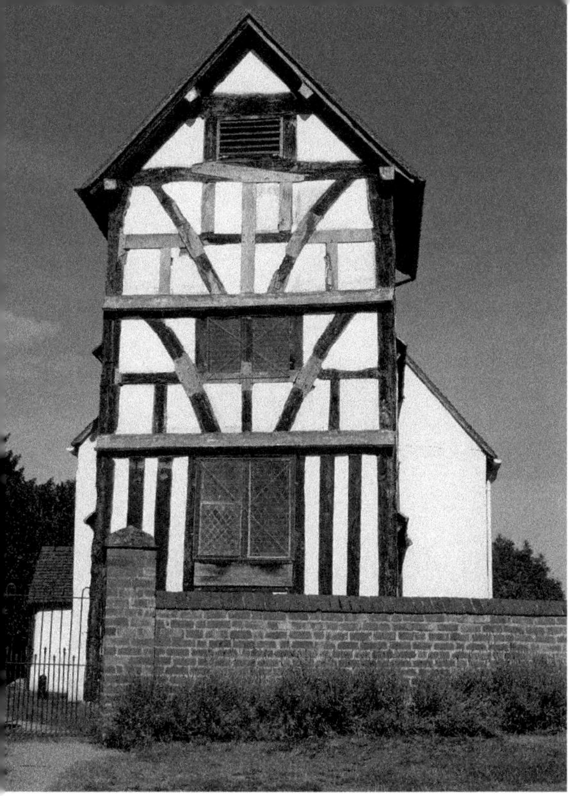

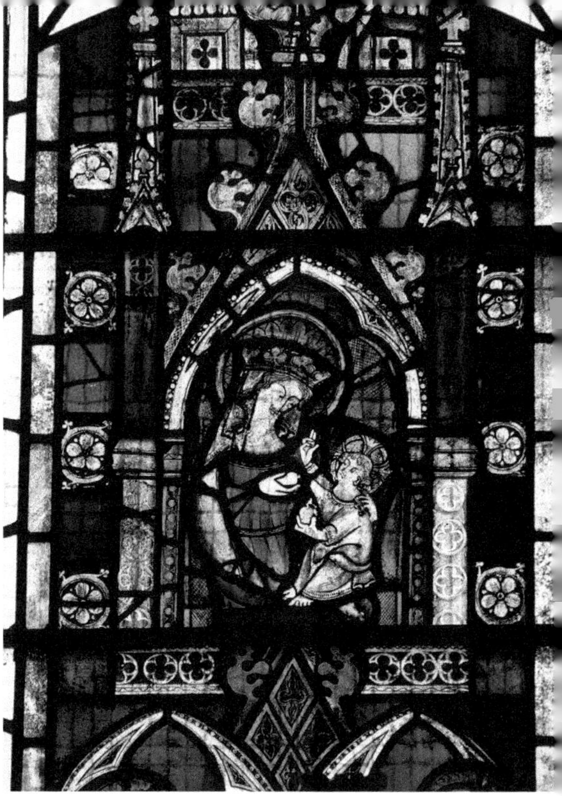

Above left: The tower of St Nicholas, Warndon, from the west.

Above right: Fourteenth-century stained glass in the east window of Warndon church.

Inside, the nave is filled by an almost complete set of early nineteenth-century box pews, which incorporate some medieval benches with poppyhead bench ends. Other medieval features are a seven-sided font, decorated floor tiles and some beautiful fourteenth- and fifteenth-century stained glass in the east window.

Part of a churchyard cross survives. The stone and brick barn next to the church has been converted into a church hall, and some of the former farm buildings have been converted into dwellings.

46. Battenhall Mount

Battenhall Mount is a remarkable house. It manages to be both a country estate in miniature and a greatly overgrown suburban villa. However, it is the quality of the late nineteenth-century craftsmanship that sets it apart.

The Battenhall area was developed for housing from the late 1850s. The gault brick and stone Italianate house here was initially built in 1865–69 for William Spriggs. In the 1890s it was bought by Alfred Percy Allsopp, brewer, MP, son of Lord Hindlip (of Hindlip Hall), and three times mayor of Worcester. Allsopp employed the architects J. H. Williams and R. A. Briggs to enlarge Spriggs' relatively modest house on a grand scale. The neighbouring house was

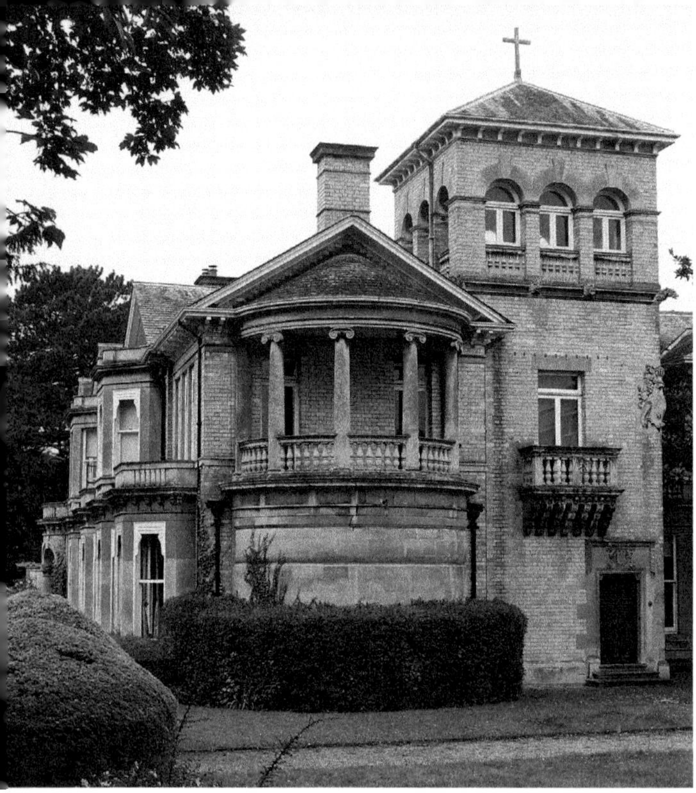

The garden front of Battenhall Mount with belvedere tower and loggia.

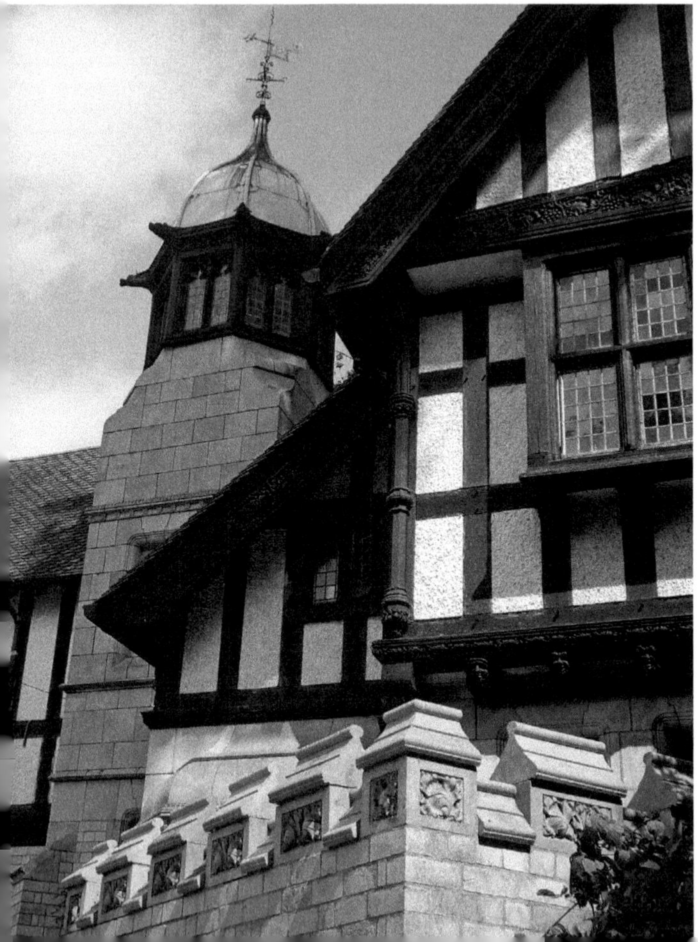

Detail of the gate lodge, Battenhall Mount.

bought and demolished to make room for an enlarged garden. A new garden wing contained a suite of reception rooms embellished with a riot of panelling, plasterwork, stone and marble carving, mosaic, tilework, stained glass and embossed leather. Artists who worked on the house are thought to have included William Forsyth, Starkie Gardner and William de Morgan, whose painted tiles of Scylla and Charybdis decorate the music room fireplace. The tiny chapel in the north wing was equally lavishly decorated, with metal screens, marquetry and inlaid stonework. Linking Spriggs' house to Allsopp's garden front is a double-height sculpture gallery decorated with carvings including portraits of Allsopp and his wife.

The house is plain towards the street, while the main frontage with balcony and loggia faces the garden and a view of the Malvern Hills. At either end there are three-storey towers; the tower over the entrance was part of Spriggs' house, while a second was added by Briggs in the 1890s.

The estate buildings are all by Williams and in a vernacular style, with liberal use of false timber framing, carved wooden bargeboards, patterned tilework, and chimneys decorated with miniature terracotta gargoyles. The main house is reached through an asymmetrical gatehouse with gates of highly decorated wrought iron. Other buildings included stables, complete with horse hospital, forge and groom's quarters, and at the far end of the garden a gardener's cottage.

Allsopp was bankrupt by 1913, and after failing to sell the house leased it as a Voluntary Aid Detachment hospital (1915–19). After the First World War it passed through a number of hands before being bought by the nuns of St Marie Madeleine Postel in 1933. They established St Mary's girls' school here, which lasted until 2014. The site is now being redeveloped for retirement homes, with all of the historic buildings retained and converted.

47. St John in Bedwardine

The medieval St John's suburb grew up around road junctions, reached from the city by a causeway across the Severn floodplain. A couple of late medieval timber-framed houses survive, along with later timber buildings and eighteenth- and nineteenth-century brick houses. At one end of the suburb was the Bull Ring, recalling the droving of livestock to market in Worcester and the 'sport' of bull-baiting, while at the other end was St John's Green, the scene of an annual hiring fair. Next to the church stands the former vicarage, which dates back to the seventeenth century.

St John's and St Cuthbert's (Lower Wick) both originated as chapelries in the very large parish of St Helen. St John in Bedwardine became the parish church for the west side of Worcester in 1371, following the closure of St Cuthbert.

The piers of the nave arcade are late twelfth century in date and are the only obvious survival of the earliest church, though the arches have been renewed, some in the fourteenth century and some in the nineteenth.

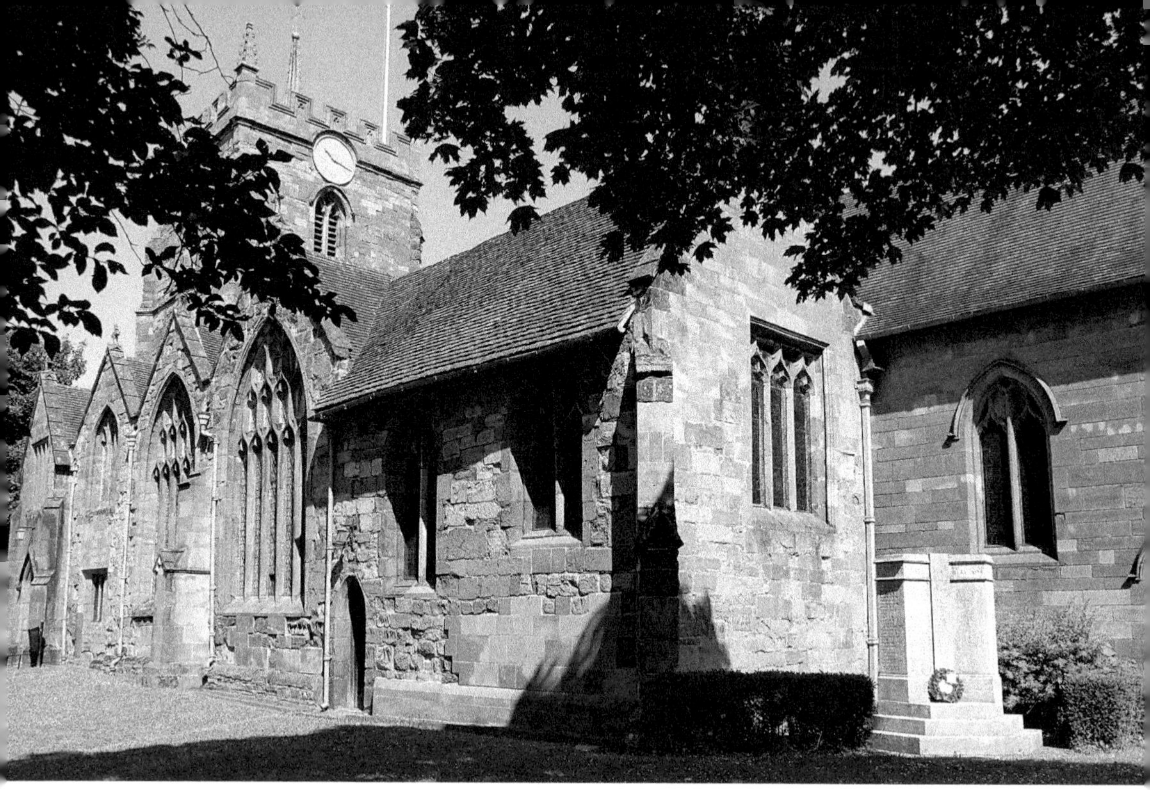

Above: St John's Church from the churchyard.

Below: The east end of St John's Church.

Inset: Heritage plaque of St John's in the Civil War by Planet Art.

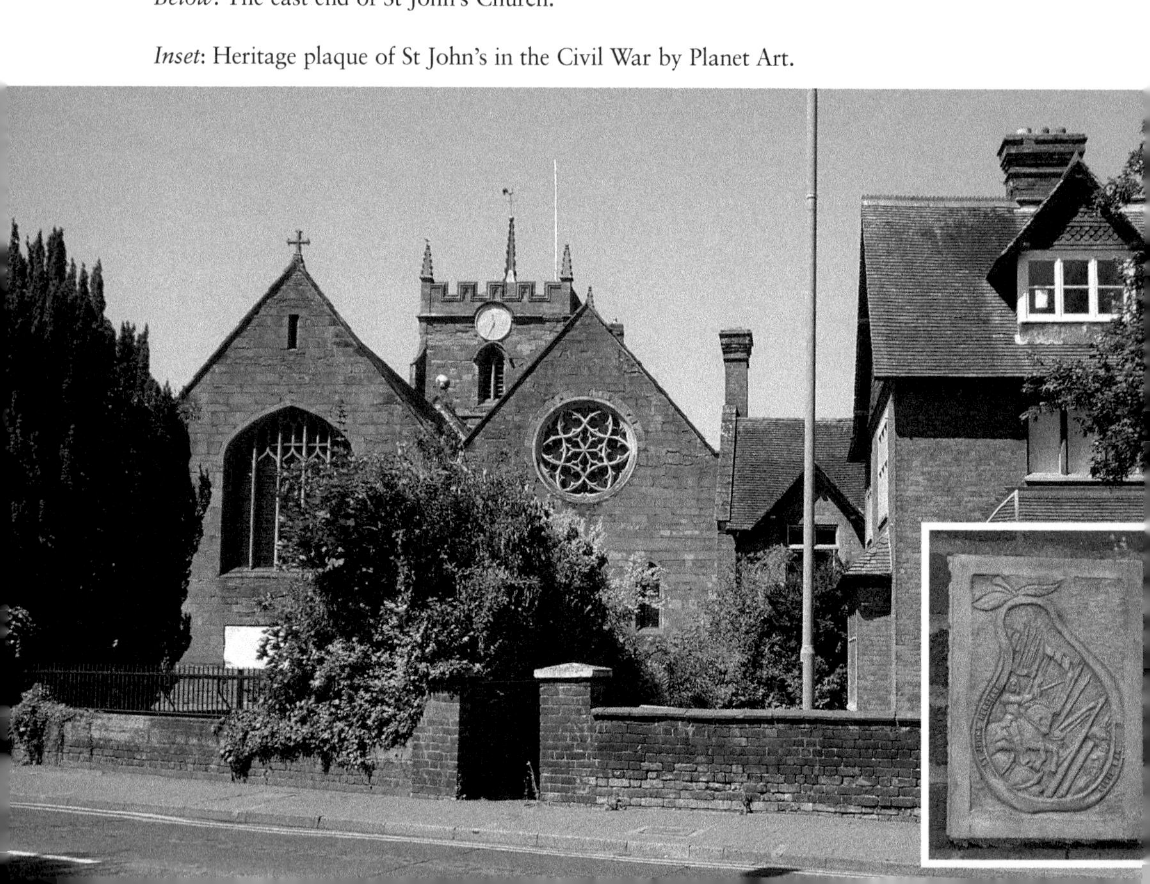

The west tower is dated 1481. Not tall, it is topped with a small fleche spire, replacing a larger spire destroyed in the Civil War. Just to the west, the besieging Parliamentary army built a siege work in 1646, and there was also action here in the Battle of Worcester.

Restoration and rebuilding in 1841 (Belling), 1861 (Perkins) and 1884 (Christian) greatly enlarged the church to the north and east, and nearly all the furnishings are of the nineteenth-century origin. In the porch is a monument of 1872 to two sons of A. M. Hopkins, which were moved here from the churchyard when the graves were cleared. Very unusually for the period, it includes a framed photograph of one of the boys.

48. St Cuthbert's Chapel

Hidden away on the edge of Worcester, behind the Manor Farm pub in Lower Wick, is St Cuthbert's Chapel. At least four phases of this little building's history can be seen in its structure.

The earliest part comprises a Norman red sandstone chapel, its fragmentary west window dating to the mid-twelfth century. The last service here was in 1371 when St Cuthbert's was replaced by St John in Bedwardine.

St Cuthbert's Chapel after restoration.

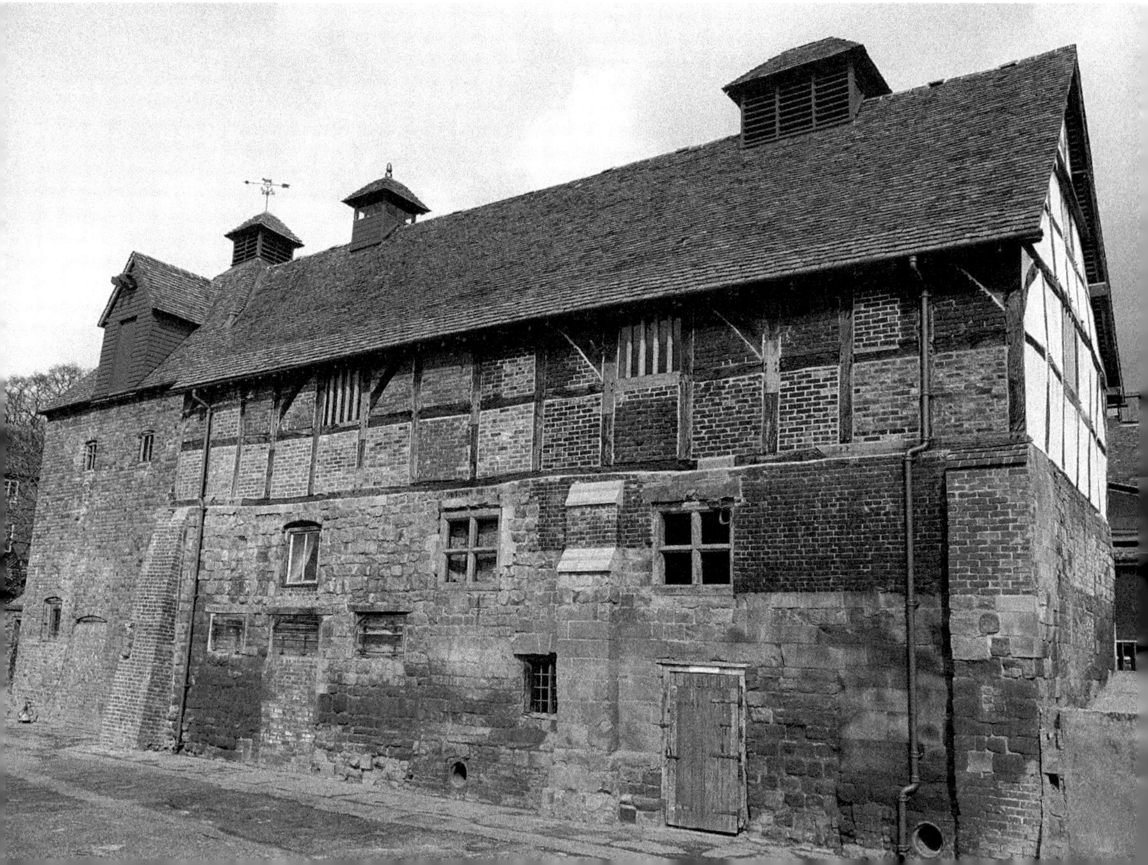

We then hear nothing about the site until the early sixteenth century, when the tenant was required to make repairs. This may relate to the square timber framing of the upper floor, tree-ring dated to between 1480 and 1530. During recent restoration the roof was stripped and over forty stamped tiles of this period were found (see The Commandery). These have only rarely been found beyond Worcester city centre. The quality of the framing and timber roof with its curved wind braces suggests a domestic use. The same goes for the ashlar stonework and mullioned windows from the seventeenth century. The chapel is said to have sheltered wounded soldiers during the Battle of Worcester, and was also used as a poorhouse.

St Cuthbert's found a new role in the mid-nineteenth century. Hop cultivation was expanding at Manor Farm, hop kilns were inserted into the old building, and a new brick store building was built at the west end. The roof vents and loading bay date from the 1850s, while inside are moveable wooden trays, extending the whole width of the building, for drying the hops.

The chapel was restored in 2012–13, but it is now redundant as a farm building and awaits a new use.

49. Powick Old Bridge

Powick Old Bridge has seen more than its share of history, and it now sits in gentle retirement, used mainly by walkers and cyclists (it is on National Cycle Route 46 from Worcester to Malvern). The patchwork of stone and brick that makes up the bridge is testament to the ravages of the Civil War as well as 400 years of use on the main road from Worcester to Malvern, before it was superseded by Powick New Bridge in 1837. It is still possible to find peace here in spite of the main roads all around.

The bridge's history is reflected in its status as the most-designated place in Worcester. The bridge is a listed building and also a scheduled monument; it sits within a conservation area and a registered historic battlefield, and the River Teme is a Site of Special Scientific Interest.

There was probably a ford here before the present bridge was built in the fifteenth century. There are really two conjoined bridges, one of three segmental skew arches crossing the Teme, the other with two round arches crossing the Laugherne Brook, which joins the Teme here. Both have substantial stone cutwaters and the parapets have angled refuges for pedestrians. The arches over the Laugherne Brook have been rebuilt in brick.

Powick Bridge featured in both the first and last battles of the Civil War. On the late afternoon of 23 September 1642 Prince Rupert's cavalry, escorting a treasure convoy that was being taken to join the Royalist army, engaged a Parliamentary cavalry force commanded by Colonel Nathaniel Fiennes. Both sides may have numbered around 1000. The Parliamentary force was routed and fled southwards

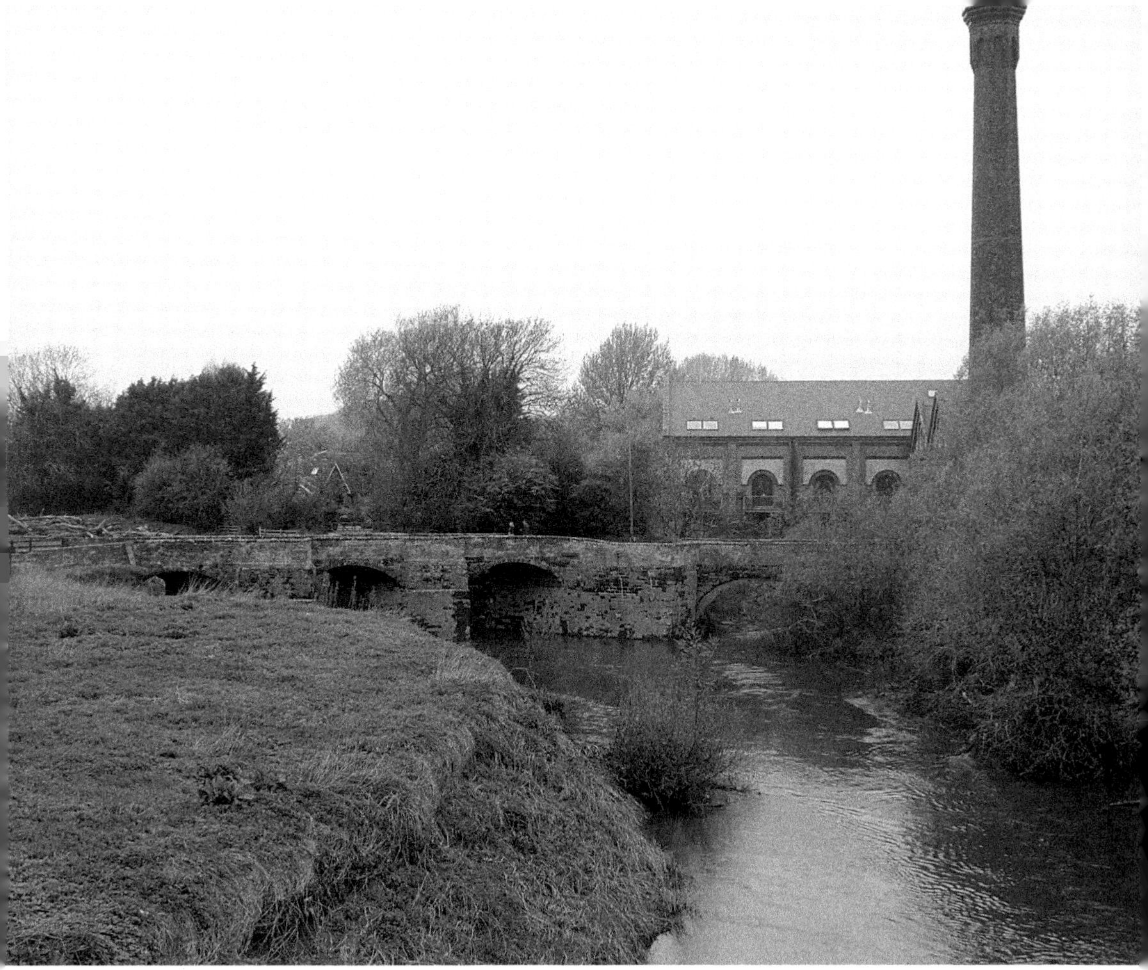

Powick Old Bridge, with Powick Mills behind.

across the bridge to join the main army. They may have lost thirty to forty men while the Royalist losses were negligible. The Battle of Powick Bridge probably lasted no longer than fifteen minutes.

The Battle of Worcester (3 September 1651) was, in contrast, one of the largest and most bloody land battles ever fought on British soil. An estimated 40,000 troops took part: 28,000 Parliamentarians of the New Model Army and 12,000 in a Royalist army made up largely of Scots. Charles II's army had spent ten days consolidating a defensive position in the city, and Powick Bridge formed part of an outer defence. It was not unusual at the time for bridges to be part-demolished for easy defence, with crossing allowed by a single plank. This is probably the reason for the rebuilding of the Laugherne Brook arches. The battle started with a Parliamentary advance under General Fleetwood from Upton and Powick. One wing of his force moved forward to Powick Bridge, but was unable to advance as the Royalist defence was solid. This had been anticipated, and instead the Parliamentary army crossed the Teme using a pre-assembled bridge of boats, close to its confluence with the Severn. They fought their way across the meadows on the north side of the Teme and were thus able to bypass Powick Bridge altogether.

50. Powick Mills

Water power has been harnessed here, on and off, for the best part of 1,000 years. The monks of Great Malvern Priory had a corn mill in 1086 and a new leat was dug between the Teme and Laughern Brook in 1475. There were two watermills here in 1543 and three in 1565. Much later a mill was grinding flint and other materials for porcelain manufacture. The Lloyd family, Quakers from mid-Wales, had an iron forge and slitting mill on the opposite bank from the 1760s (the stream bank is still revetted with iron hearth bottoms). Other members of this enterprising family gave their name to Lloyds Bank.

The present building opened in 1894 as the City of Worcester Electricity Works, the first municipal hydro-electric power station in Britain. The Teme, which lends water to the little Laughern Brook via the 'New Cut' just upstream (an enlarged version of the medieval leat), is not a reliable river, and there was a very low head of water. Hence a steam engine was also provided to ensure a constant electricity supply, and the octagonal chimney is a well-known landmark, visible from the city centre as well as the nearby roads. There were three steam engines and four water turbines. The 400 kw generating capacity was no doubt large at the time, but nowadays would be enough to supply just sixty households.

The electricity works pediment at Powick Mills.

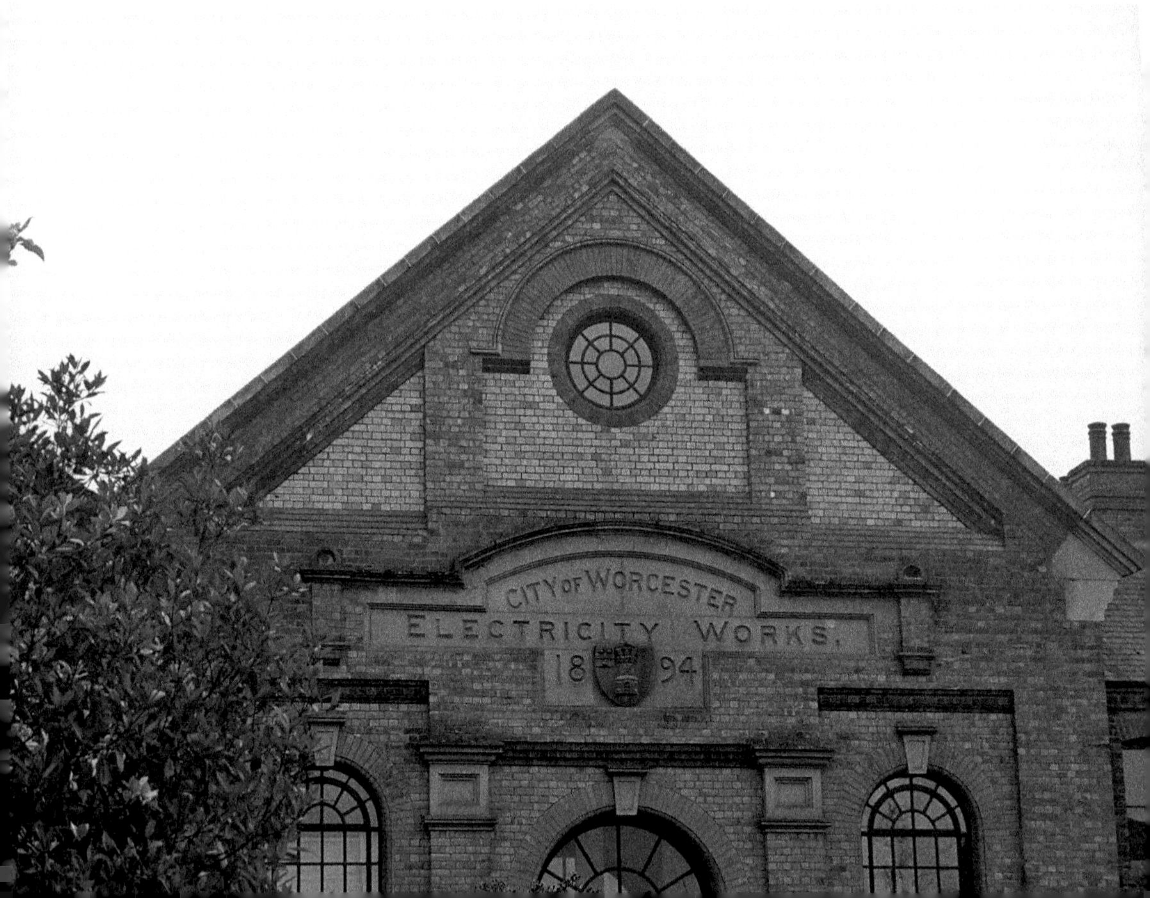

Powick Mills and chimney from the Old Bridge.

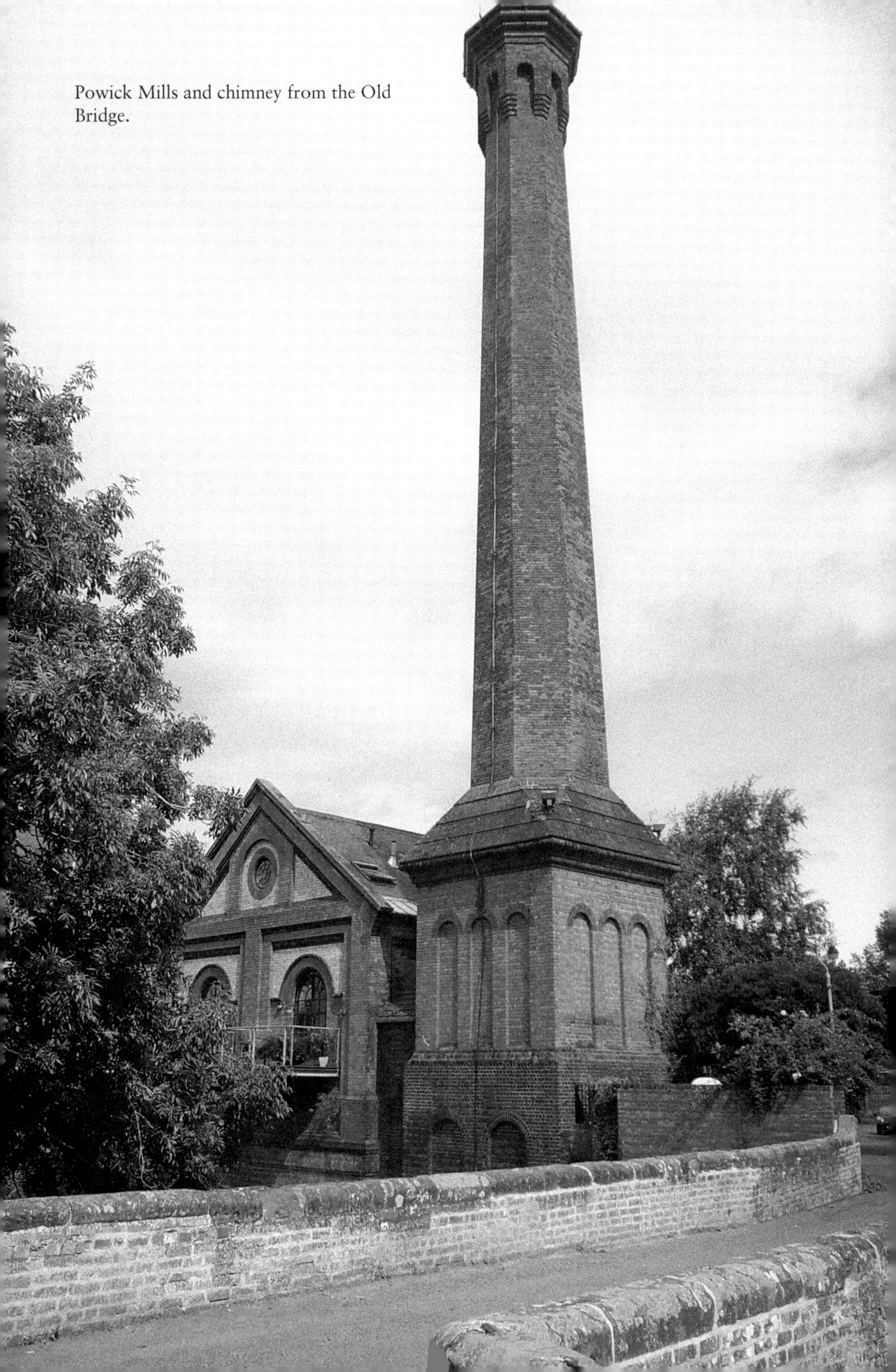

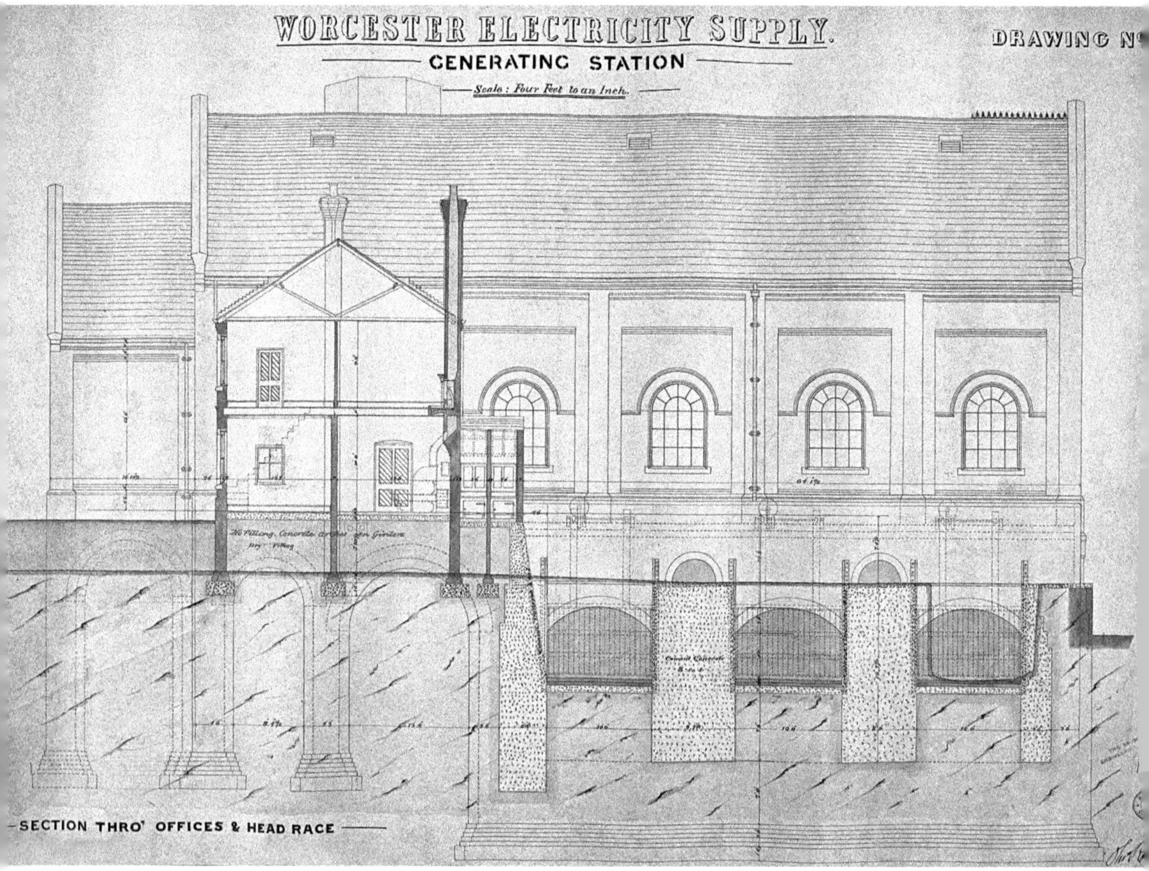

Power station building plan, 1893. (Worcester City Archives)

When Worcester's tram network started to develop around 1900, the Powick electricity works was supplemented by a much larger coal-fired power station on the Severn bank in central Worcester. Shortly afterwards, steam generation ceased, though the works continued as a hydro-electric station until the late 1920s. The building then became a water-driven laundry into the 1950s. Sadly no use is now made of the water power. None of the machinery survives apart from a travelling crane, now moved outside and displayed next to the small car park. The building has been preserved and was converted into housing in 1999.

Bibliography

Atkin, M., *Cromwell's Crowning Mercy: The Battle of Worcester, 1651* (Stroud: Sutton, 1998)

Baker, N. J., and Holt, R . A., *Urban Growth and the Medieval Church: Gloucester and Worcester* (Farnham: Ashgate Publishing, 2004)

Barker, P. A., Guy, C., and Romain, C., *Worcester Cathedral: A Short History* (3rd edition) (Almeley: LogastonPress , 2007)

Bridges, T., *The Churches of Worcestershire* (2nd edition) (Almeley: Logaston Press, 2005)

Bridges, T., and Mundy, C. F., *Worcester: A Pictorial History* (Hambledon: Phillimore, 1996)

Brooks, A., and Pevsner, N., *The Buildings of England: Worcestershire* (Yale University Press, 2007)

Engel, U., *Worcester Cathedral: An Architectural History* (Bognor Regis: Phillimore, 2007)

Green, V., *The History and Antiquities of the City and Suburbs of Worcester* (1796)

Hughes, P. M., and Leech, A., *The Story of Worcester* (Almeley: Logaston, 2011)

Whitehead, D., *The Book of Worcester* (Barracuda Books, 1979)

Worcester City Historic Environment Record, available at Heritage Gateway: https://www.heritagegateway.org.uk/gateway/

The Changing Face of Worcester: http://www.cfow.org.uk/

National Heritage List for England: https://historicengland.org.uk/listing/the-list/

Acknowledgements

My thanks go to very many people who have taught me over the years. Owners of buildings and other keyholders have been unfailingly helpful in showing me building interiors and allowing photography. I am grateful to Chris Dobbs for the use of his image of the Guildhall, a notoriously difficult building to photograph. Sheena Payne-Lunn and Pat Hughes have provided much valuable information on buildings and images. Finally I thank my family, who have put up with my working on this book for rather longer than anyone expected.